The Return of the Gods

American University Studies

Series V
Philosophy

Vol. 78

PETER LANG
New York • Bern • Frankfurt am Main • Paris

Frederick Sontag

The Return of the Gods

A Philosophical/Theological Reappraisal of the Writings of Ernest Becker

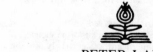

PETER LANG
New York • Bern • Frankfurt am Main • Paris

Library of Congress Cataloging-in-Publication Data

Sontag, Frederick
 The return of the gods : a philosophical/theological
reappraisal of the writings of Ernest Becker / Frederick
Sontag.
 p. cm. — (American university studies. Series V,
Philosophy ; vol. 78)
1. Social sciences — Religious aspects — Christianity
— History of doctrines — 20th century. 2. Gods —
Miscellanea. 3. Becker, Ernest. 4. Death.
5. Alienation (Philosophy) 6. Meaning (Philosophy)
I. Title. II. Series.
BRl15.S57S67 1989 233'.092'4. — dcl9 88-30501
ISBN 0-8204-0909-X   CIP
ISSN 0739-6392

CIP-Titelaufnahme der Deutschen Bibliothek

Sontag, Frederick:
The return of the Gods : a philosophical-theolo-
gical reappraisal of the writings of Ernest Becker
/ Frederick Sontag. — New York; Bern; Frankfurt
am Main; Paris: Lang, 1989.
 (American University Studies: Ser. 5,
 Philosophy, Vol. 78)
 ISBN 0-8204-0909-X

NE: American University Studies / 05

© Peter Lang Publishing, Inc., New York 1989

Printed by Weihert-Druck GmbH, Darmstadt, West Germany

OTHER BOOKS BY FREDERICK SONTAG

With John K. Roth

> *The American Religious Experience: The Roots, Trends and Future of
>   American Theology, 1972*
> *God and America's Future, 1977*
> *The Defense of God, eds., 1985*
> *The Questions of Philosophy, 1988*

Frederick Sontag

> *Divine Perfection: Possible Ideas of God, 1962*
> *The Existentialist Prolegomena: To a Future Metaphysics, 1969*
> *The Future of Theology: A Philosophical Basis for Contemporary Protestant
>   Theology, 1969*
> *The Crisis of Faith: A Protestant Witness in Rome, 1969*
> *The God of Evil: An Argument for the Existence of the Devil, 1970*
> *God, Why Did You Do That? 1970*
> *The Problems of Metaphysics, 1970*
> *How Philosophy Shapes Theology: Problems in the Philosophy of Religion,
>   1971*
> *Love Beyond Pain: Mysticism within Christianity, 1977*
> *Sun Myung Moon and the Unification Church, 1977*
> *What Can God Do? 1979*
> *A Kierkegaard Handbook, 1979*
> *The Elements of Philosophy, 1984*
> *Emotion: Its Role in Understanding and Decision, 1989*

For

L. B. K.

She listened to us, and
the Lord opened her heart
to accept what Paul was
saying.

Acts 16:14
The Jerusalem Bible

The spiritual decline of the earth is so far advanced that the nations are in danger of losing the last bit of spiritual energy that makes it possible to see the decline...the flight of the gods...

Martin Heidegger
An Introduction to Metaphysics

"We all applauded, tearfully; these were the Gods returning after a centuries-long exile."

Jorge Luis Borges, "Ragnarok"
Labyrinths

TABLE OF CONTENTS

INTRODUCTION

To announce the return of the Gods presupposes that they have departed. Furthermore, to speak of "the Gods" means that we are speaking of more than one deity, or at least more than one way in which God can be present to us. If the ways in which Deity appears, then, are multiple, that is, if the theophanies are many, this helps us understand our situation. One God, or one form of God's appearance, can disappear and even be absent for a considerable period of time, and God can still be present to other times and places. Having said this, we must admit that if all Gods have not been absent in recent times, still religion in general and God in particular have been under attack since the Modern Age began. The advancement of science seemed to many to require that the Gods be banned in the interest of pressing the age of science to its full maturity. All humanity, it was thought, would benefit from the absence of the Gods. Under the direction of science, humanity could develop more fully when not restrained by divinities who transcend nature.

It seemed to many in this new age that, if nature was to be explored and human potential developed to its fullest, the Gods should not be allowed to interfere. Deities often called us to think of other worlds and to explore realms beyond us, but all our energy was needed to explore nature fully now that the scientific tools to do so were in our hands at last. Prometheus had won. The result was that simple people might retain religious superstition, but any intellectual who was captivated by the Enlightenment had to reject the Gods in order to find solidarity in the quest to release humanity from age old bonds once and for all. The educated and intellectual class turned away from all Gods as a mark of intelligence. Under Marx's guidance, the proletariat joined the intelligentsia in rejecting all transcendental beings in the revolutionary zeal to improve the economic conditions of the poor. The Gods were reduced to being lower middle class Deities; all the while they were attacked from both sides in the name of improving the human lot.

Of course, here and there and from time to time, the Gods counterattacked, rising up from our collective unconscious, as Jung might say, captivating masses and arousing religious fervor as they had in the old days of religious imperialism. Still, the intellectuals and masses of workers who were in revolt stayed aloof or mocked those who fell back into their old ways as not being dedicated to human advance. And so the Gods could never fully regain the old place of respect they enjoyed in the Middle Ages when kings bent to religious commands and philosophers were theologians automatically. The retreat of the Gods was simultaneous with the future independence of the Social Sciences and the destruction of the Ptolemaic system. After all, physics and mathematics were only intended to provide the base, but the completion of the humanistic revolution depended on providing a scientific social base. If the rising power of science was to transform humankind, a new science of humanity had to be erected on that base to complete the human reconstruction. Many claimed that weak human beings had in ages past needed religion in order to cope with human ills. Religion had sustained the slaves in America quite well. But once the modern revolution had been completed, it was asserted, humankind could take charge of its own destiny through the rise of the Social Sciences.

True, not every revolutionary shared exactly the same program for human reconstruction. Comte was not Marx. But all did share in the exhilarating prospect of liberating humankind and in believing that it was only a matter of time until all sciences were united on a world-wide basis. How could anyone with intelligence not be captivated by such a prospect? Patently, the emergence of humans-on-their-own was a novel prospect, after who knows how many centuries of being bent to the service of often terrifying Deities. And this program was not the dream of some wild visionary, like those prophets and messiahs who had so often roused our religious fervor. It was all to be based on the bedrock of a rising science and the human control of nature's immense powers now released for our use. It became a test of intelligence to see if one was strong enough to reject the support of religious rituals. For many, to explore the nature of God was no longer a mark of intelligence. Religion became superstition. Theology was no longer queen of the sciences. The queen was dead; long live the new-born Social Sciences! Surely only the weak could refuse such a call.

With such a heady prospect before us, how could anyone expect the Gods ever to return? Their absence had to be permanent if great goals were to be accomplished. This was also the age of belief in continual cumulative progress. Once launched, the upward spiral could never turn back again. Humanity had reached a point of no return, and who could tell how far we might go once the reins of science were in our hands? Time and history were on our side. Who of any strength could return to a time of God-dependence? We knew the natural impulse we all-too-human beings had to sin, but now we had a chance to rise above sin and foreswear begging God's forgiveness. To do all this we first had to revise human nature so that it would no longer be what it once was. Thus, the rise of the Social Sciences was crucial to the whole scenario. Without the remaking of human nature, the power released by the evolving Natural Sciences might come to naught as far as the improvement of the human condition was concerned.

Why should any thinking person consider the return of the Gods? With democracy rising up as a political option, "Keep out anything which transcends nature so that we can complete the conquest of nature unobstructed!"--was the cry. Physicians were busy reconstructing human bodies and relieving pain in ways undreamed of only a short while before.

Why not remold human nature to match and complete the job? One needed not to be a Marxist to believe that the dialectic of history was driving us forward, since the Marxist doctrine was not unique; it was merely one form of the growing confidence in our ability to transform humankind. We could now resurrect ourselves from the tombs that had held us captive for centuries. With this in prospect, how do we dare announce the return of the Gods? Anyone with intelligence, it seems, would give anything to keep them banished and in exile from our thought so that the work could be completed. The Gods now seemed to threaten our whole human dream, rather than being its fulfillment as once had been believed.

The whole issue, I believe, hinges on assessing the success of the failure of the Social Sciences in achieving their goals for us. The results of the conquests of Natural Science are indisputable and obvious enough to all. We fly, we replace the human heart, we travel in space, and we talk to each other across vast distances with amazing clarity. Yet we require a new human nature to match all these advances. There is no great advantage if the women and men who guide the space ships and talk to one another via satellite are human beings prone to sin. In spite of all our dreams of human glory and our science-founded confidence, an increasing sense of uneasiness has gripped the twentieth century. Ours is still a century of terror and violence, not peace. True, Marx told us that violent revolution was necessary first to break the old bonds and release humankind. In spite of the changes wrought by some revolutions, the French and the Russian for two, there is little confidence abroad that revolutions always break old fetters. An increasing fear is abroad that violence only breeds new tyrants.

Therefore, we need to re-examine the proposed revolution of the Social Sciences. If this revolution fails, our new-born human hope to achieve final release stands in question and the Gods wait in the wings, alert for the cry of the suffering human soul to call them forth once more. Either we must prove that it lies within our power to save ourselves as we promised, or else we must license the return of all contenders for the role of savior. But if we are to carry out such an important reappraisal of these now several centuries old great human hopes, why should we turn to the writings of Ernest Becker? Because he understands fully the metaphysical premises of the Social Sciences, shares their early hope to transform humankind, is clinically aware of their failures to do so to date, but is still optimistic of their chance to do so now. He has his own program to explain how that which has eluded us for centuries can finally be placed within our grasp, and at the same time he is sensitive to the natural disposition of the human soul to religious belief.

Others who heralded the rise of the new age and the exile of the Gods thought our cities would become fully secular in short order. And to all apostles of the age of scientific secularism, any outcropping of religious sentiment is an embarrassment and a threat to the desired transformation. For this reason secular societies, whether Marxist or humanist, often oppose religion and tend to suppress it as a threat to the state, which in a sense it is. Yet in the United States we have consistently experienced waves of religious revivalism and have come to accept them as natural. And the same stir appears abroad. In America this happens because we are cross-breeds. We are at once religiously born and at the same time sons and daughters of the belief in progress and in our ability to create a society that escapes the old tendency to decadence. Many Americans still hold on to their confidence in the Social Sciences to aid us in this noble project. For these reasons, an American writer may provide the best source for our reappraisal of the goals of the Social Sciences. Each of the following chapters analyzes Becker's extended review of the goals of the Social Sciences and asks: Are we about to regroup to achieve what has eluded us in two centuries of pursuit, as he hopes; or is it time to pronounce the revolution unsuccessful and welcome the Gods back once more? In any case, we must warn the reader in advance that not every person who is religiously disposed, whether Christian, Hebrew, or Muslim, will rejoice in our conclusion, since it does not welcome back one God but rather many divinities. And it was partly because the Gods were so varied and religions so competitive that many wanted all banned as divisive for the anthropological, i.e., human-centered, age. True, religious wars were and are vicious, so there is no reason to suppose that the return of the Gods will be the age of human harmony Marx wanted to achieve with the classless society. But do we have any choice, if in fact the Social Sciences have not produced the unity and transformation of human nature so long sought?

In order to decide this, follow Ernest Becker's intellectual odyssey as outlined in the succeeding brief chapters. His vision of our offer of a new future is thrilling, but it is also tragic if it is not to be. See if, after two centuries of false starts, you can along with Becker rekindle your own optimism that we still can do it if we will regroup our forces and unite. And if you think his revised agenda can no more succeed than the original project to remodel humanity, do you hear the Gods returning? If so, are the old wars we sought to avoid also to be part of this return, and has humanity progressed so little intellectually beyond the time of origins? Furthermore, what must revolutionaries do now if their militant secularism cannot be sustained? What goals must intelligence set for itself, if the ban on the Gods cannot be continued for all intelligent people, or even for all dedicated revolutionaries?

The "Dark Ages" were perhaps not so dark as Enlightenment prejudice and the optimism of scientific hopes made out. The Middle Ages were not quite "medieval" as theories of Progress once supposed. Still, no one really wants the bonds we have loosened to be reimposed. Democracy offers some virtues which exceed living defenselessly under royal tyrants. We have achieved a measure of human rights, even if fragile and partial; must these be trampled under foot if the Gods return? It would seem so, if we observe some new rising theocracies which suppresses freedom in the name of one

God or another. However, the crucial factor here is whether the return of the divine is of one tyrannical God or of many. "There is safety in numbers," we say, and the same is true of the company of the Gods. If we admit that divinities remain multiple, we can reject the tyranny of anyone who claims to speak in the name of some exclusive God's return who would sweep out all opposition before one set of divine demands. No human being, then, can claim exclusive divine representation and persecute all non-conformists. This present return of the Gods must be plural, non-conformist, and protective of every human right gained in their absence.

This is why we should examine and appraise the works of Ernest Becker as a symbol of our age. If he is right, the Gods' return must be delayed while we try once more to carry out the reform of humanity, as well as the banishment of both evil and all transcendence. As the world reels under violence today, acting as if it had not changed much, all the while the Gods can be heard approaching, we must decide either to try Becker's revised program of reform or to admit that we have returned to our origins.

Of course, as far as the future is concerned, we have to ask if the same Gods can all return? Or, does some of what we have learned in the Modern Age demand a reform in divinities, even if human nature cannot, as we hoped, be totally revolutionized? After all, since the Gods have always been metamorphosed in history, there is no reason to think new divinities will not arise. If we once proposed to banish the Gods because they thwarted human progress, and if our analysis of Becker's ban lets us concur in the Gods' return, we should ask: What nature of divinity is most conducive to human fulfillment? As we give answers to this question, we should be sure that such a God is among the Gods admitted. If, on the other hand, any divinity terrorizes humanity, we could still agree to keep such a one in exile in the name of human freedom. Can we now elect our Gods democratically? That is our question.

CHAPTER I

ANTHROPODICY OR THEODICY?[1]

Evil is a problem in every era, particularly for religion and theology. If one struggles with God, whether personally or intellectually, it is also difficult to account for the way Gods deals with man. However, the rise of the Social Sciences is coordinate with the rejection of theodicy and proposes that, in the world of Modern Science, anthropodicy should replace theodicy. That is, if we work to develop a science of humanity, we should be able to deal with evil on a purely human level, thus leaving God and the supernatural out of this accounting. A more radical suggestion would eliminate speaking about "evil" altogether. It would do so on the grounds that the term "evil" is religiously tainted. We should speak only of human fault or error and of our programs for their correction. It is an important event, then, when a social theorist devotes a major effort to examining evil in its relation to the program

---

[1]This chapter was originally presented in an earlier form as a paper for the XIVth International Congress of the International Association for the History of Religions, meeting at Winnipeg, Canada, August 17-21, 1980.

of the Social Sciences.[2]

Becker is convinced that "something very serious is wrong with our science" (p. ix) today, and he connects this fault with the problem of evil. The rise of the Social Sciences involves denying theodicy and making the claim that humanity can handle evil as an anthropodicy, that is, accounting for it in entirely human terms. Thus, the complaint about the failure of the Social Sciences to carry out their proposed program is tied to the problem of evil. The "science of humanity" we sought and needed has not been produced, Becker asserts. Becker thinks that this should make psychology less hostile to philosophy than it once was (p. x). The rationalism of the Enlightenment wanted to do away with the religious basis for unity in the Middle Ages, and also with its tendency to punish heretics, but complete rationalism serves the intellectuals only, not the rest of society (p. 6). Science and the needs of human life were not reconciled by the Enlightenment.

Saint-Pierre held that humanity should consciously plan a better future by applying social science to human affairs. This is the goal. If it is accepted, outlining an anthropodicy and correcting evil is our primary concern. Certainly God is not important if power over nature is now in humanity's hands. If humanity is the center from which all the sciences radiate, we need

---

[2]Ernest Becker, The Structure of Evil, Free Press, New York, 1976. All page references are to this edition.

no longer be burdened by other-worldliness. Within the church, humanity knew right from wrong. Yet, even as religion became less central to life, a sensitivity to the problem of evil remained. When God no longer introduced a note of awe, good and evil became "merely an affair of technical calculation" (p. 17). Humanity did need a new theodicy. But unfortunately, we also could no longer put the burden on God. Ours must be a theodicy without divine intervention. What resulted was a "limited anthropodicy, that is, not an explanation of all evils but only those that allow a human remedy.

This shift from a God-centered to a human-centered interpretation succeeds as long as evil can be effectively confined. Since anthropodicy limits evil, if it should prove that we cannot remove all tragic loss, we are back to the problem of evil. That is, evil as the destruction of life beyond human capacity to remedy. However, the weakness in the Social Science approach lies in its tendency to accommodate to the social world even while pretending to reform it. Hume wanted to build a new secular morality, but by now we have given up the project to build a science of humanity. Diderot too saw the need for a new secular morality, but he could provide no solution. In a subtle way this is connected to the notion of a gradual evolution, or the secular "idea of progress" (p. 26). We hoped that an irreversible movement forward would rehabilitate humanity in spite of nature.

Rousseau wanted humanity to give morality the status of a basic science, to find the law within human nature based on humanity as it is. But the problems involved are many, and Rousseau's proposal is complicated. For instance, does this approach allow us to build a program to regenerate nature? What if there is no law within human nature sufficient to generate a morality? And, if evil is endemic, can its explanation be found without God? The task of the science of humanity is to change society. Humans should choose and create the kind of world they want, it was said. But all this assumes that evil is not such that it will thwart carrying out the plan. Humanity must liberate itself. This is a fully secular theodicy, an anthropodicy, but it is based on the possibility of humanity achieving freedom from destructive evil. Perhaps the French Revolution failed; if so, was that a failure of reason or the failure not to give reason enough sway in human affairs?

This is the dilemma that plagues us in trying to assess the modern hope to build an anthropodicy on a science of humanity and dispense with theodicy. The new society has not emerged free from the evils of human destruction. Yet is this because the program of the Social Sciences is faulty in its assumptions, or is it because it has not yet been carried far enough? We have had three centuries of trying social reform to eliminate evil. Humanists want us to close ranks and make another try. "This time we'll do it," they say, rather than to return to any God as an explanation of our fault. Yet the suspicion grows that it isn't in our power to alter human nature so radically, even if individuals can be improved. We need models of dignity and excellence if we are to pursue goals of change, but can they come from the human plane?

Freedom has been enhanced but not without increased destruction. The art of enslavement has been refined so that it is as much a danger now as in the days of legal slavery. Responsibility has faded as a virtue, and community life suffers when everyone lives for his or her own pursuits. Often we say we want democracy because it is the birthmark of modern humanism, but have we failed to lay the groundwork for real democracy? We blame education, but is our failure due to too little or too much education? All the while the moral fiber of society deteriorates. Comte wanted to replace the lost medieval morality with a new scientific and moral synthesis. If theodicy is ruled out, this substitution must take place or else all morality becomes haphazard. If you can extend rational, scientific analysis into all domains, you have an anthropodicy. But what is the evidence of our success in attempting to found an adequate morality on this basis?

There is hardly a voice which does not speak to the decay of morality in our time. But if the thesis of an anthropodicy is based on building a substitute morality, our failures should cause us to re-examine the program of anthropodicy. Where morality is concerned, it makes all the difference in how we construct morality as to where we pinpoint the explanation of the evil that destroys humanity. Doing away with God was partly promised on the assumption that we can account for evil and also control and even eradicate it on our own. Comte had the vision of active social change as something humanly achievable. The United States was founded partly on such an assumption too. But we flounder. We need to rethink just how much ever-recurring evil holds us back from making the "final change."

As we begin to realize what assumptions lie behind "the science of humanity" and anthropodicy and hold these up against the decay in modern society, we should ask? Is that age now gone, and are we living in a time of "the return of the Gods"? True, one reason for the Humanists' revolt was the inadequacy of the medieval visions of God for the dawning age of science. If theodicy is to return, it should come with concepts of God more fitting to the age of scientific achievement and control. The notion of "human progress" was one of the basic assumptions of anthropodicy, modern history shows it was a false assumption. If in order to understand ourselves fully we must finalize the laws of human nature before we can organize a true modern society, then, we ask: What evidence is there that such a science is possible?

Have we simply shirked the central task of a science of humanity, the active implementation of human progress, as Becker postulates? Or is it the case that anthropodicy is able to account for some human destruction but not for all? "The moral promise of commercial-industrial society has literally become ashes--and in our time, in Bushenwald and in Hiroshima," Becker reports (p. 62). Marx, of course, spoofed the visions and plans of the utopian socialists stressing that socialism must be scientific from the beginning. He was partly right, but is this as he thought because anthropodicy and human progress are viable if allied with science and not with utopian vision. Marx was an Enlightenment figure too. He rejected the bourgeois variety of the idea of progress. Parliamentary democracy, he believed, could not solve the problems of the industrial society. But on the other hand has his radical program to reconstruct society by revolution fulfilled the hope of anthropodicy any more? Has evil and destruction been contained within human bounds? The holocausts of Germany, Russia, China, and Cambodia would seem to say no.

Is our problem only that we must find another anthropodicy and its idea of human progress which can succeed where the other versions have failed? Marx correctly spotted new sources of human alienation, but does his formula eradicate all sources of alienation or just certain forms? Marx saw the perfectibility of humanity and human progress as an automatic law of history, aided by the continual class struggle. But what if class conflict is real but still is not the sole law of development so that history is subject to continual loss? Marx was dogmatic about his metaphysical assumptions, because he genuinely believed them to be based on the sole theory modern science would validate. Yet science has turned out to be anything but singular and does not dictate one program as Marx hoped.

If our future is open and flexible, unfortunately there is nothing inevitable about progress or human improvement or the eradication of evil. Marx drew "the veil of nineteenth-century mechanistic scientism over the science of man" (p. 67), but what about our account of evil if science has not eliminated it but rather expanded its scope? All hope of a unifying, active moral vision, which anthropodicy requires as a premise, dies. If we abandon the drive to moral reform of modern sociology and treat it as a science in the service of no one program what function does it have? What was originally animated by a dream becomes disoriented when the vision fades. If, as a science, sociology can provide no absolute laws of human nature, it has no key to solving of social problems because it has repudiated its own original thesis.

Why did all the schools of Sociology of the nineteenth and twentieth centuries fail to carry out their programs of reform? And the same could be asked about psychology and the other Social Sciences. A sentimental philanthropic aim brought them into existence. As they became pure sciences, Becker admits; they abandoned the goal of "making human life all that it is capable of becoming" (p.86). What then justifies their existence if we give up the assumption that human nature is governed by inevitable laws which we can discover and control? The much-lauded unity of the sciences in the service of humanity did not materialize. That hope was partly etched to a disciplinary quest, but were its assumptions in anthropodicy justified? Sociology became a science of sorts, but it lost its goal to outline human nature on purely scientific grounds.

Why belabor this point? Only a few in any of the Social Sciences still expect their early grandiose plans to be carried out. Most Social Scientists are glad to be rid of the crusading quasi-religious zeal of the high expectation to transform humanity and are only too glad to settle for being a quiet, fact-gathering "science" of a lesser sort. Our problem is not so much the change in the basic assumptions of the Social Sciences, although that is important, as it is to explain the revival of religious consciousness after the Social Sciences sought to eliminate or transform it. In particular, our awareness of evil has recently become central. For religion and theology, and for humanity in general, it is important that the project to control evil through anthropodicy has failed. And could it be that treating evil again as a religious problem goes hand in hand with the revival of religious sensitivity? If so, the Gods return precisely when evil lies close at hand, not when it is banished.

In contrast, Ernest Becker admits that the early programs of the Social Sciences failed, but he still thinks that a science of humanity has been produced. He believes that it has solved the problem of what makes people do what they do. If so, it has produced what the Enlightenment saw as crucial, an anthropodicy. Now can we be liberated from the constraints of society. "Here is a structure of thought that mankind might conceivably use for its own liberation, for the creation of a new kind of man in a new society" (p. 98). But how can Becker document the failure of every early program among the Social Sciences and still think the key lies there? If the final agreed science of humanity which allows us to be transformed cannot be produced, evil cannot be escaped today anymore than before. An anthropodicy cannot be written, because we cannot find the key to human nature that allows us to liberate all peoples. Freud proposed his solution which would have phased out religion.

Is there anything in the history of the Social Sciences to date which justifies Becker's confidence that they have produced a science of humanity about which all can agree, since universal agreement is necessary to reconstruct human nature? Certainly not, judging by the mixed reception of his own theories. Of course, he could be right, in spite of being largely ignored, but the plan to explain evil with an anthropodicy and liberate all does rest on the assumption that we can get agreement on a science of humanity. If basic disagreements about theory remain, we can propose theories but the final reform cannot be carried out, other than by enforced conformity. Becker thinks that the great achievement of the nineteenth-century was "the uniting of the empiricist and the idealist approaches into one synthetic whole" (p. 101). This would be a happy result if true. But where is the evidence that this has occurred other than on the pages of a book? It is declared to be accomplished but only words justify the hope.

The science of humanity had its principles of consciousness which permit us to understand all the mysteries of the human world, Becker argues. The problem is that the "understanding" this produces is theory-dependent.

One who does not accept the theory fully, or who uses a different theory for interpretation, will not necessarily find all the mysteries explained.

Comte thought that "human history is the record of the development of human intelligence toward greater freedom and control" (p. 103). But such a statement stems from his basic beliefs and not from a neutral science. Value is injected into nature from an anthropocentric position. Can we reach agreement to do this, or do we surrender all hope for uniformity if we introduce values? The result is that neither science or philosophy now aspires to give us wisdom. For all human beings, it seems that wisdom must include a comprehensive picture of evil. Is a philosophical unification of thought both necessary and possible? It must be, if there is to be an anthropodicy. And there must be an agreed anthropodicy, that is, a knowledge of the sources of evil and a formula for their control within human nature, if humanity is to reform himself and society. The problem is that proposals for unity and for the "final solution" to philosophical differences arise while very little unity of theory develops. In some schemes, and in the minds of some, such unity is said to be either achieved or possible, and yet no such unity takes place in fact. Communism has fought bitterly to keep its theory uniform, but even force and violence do not seem to have succeeded in keeping intellectual dissidence from breaking out as is true of all dogmas. Is part of the recent rise of violence in society due to our frustration in not being able to unite all theory, all the while we know that the success of any fundamental reform depends on doing so? Ironically, evil and destruction break out in the very attempt to eliminate evil from human society.

If we have a complete theory of human development, Becker argues, we can use it to analyze human ills. We already have many such theories, but there is no evidence that we have, or will ever agree on, one theory or that humanity is in the process of being cured by any one. For example, "alienation" is said to be a peculiarly modern problem, and Marx offers us one important theory of its origin and cure. If one is estranged from his own life activity, he or she is estranged from others and from a world in which one should be creatively involved. Social psychology may also be able to reveal to us the social sources of alienation. There is nothing wrong with multiple explanations except that only a partial cure of some individuals is possible within any pluralism, not the transformation of society as a whole. But if we insist on explaining human nature by referring to the social conditions to which we are subjected, we assume that: (1) these conditions do explain us fully, and that (2) human nature is not fixed but capable of becoming many things within society.

At this point we have touched the nerve of the problem of evil in modern times. If our nature is not fixed but reflects our social conditions, and thus may be altered by changing these conditions, evil can (at least theoretically) be eliminated. But if we carry within ourselves not only the seeds of greatness but also the seeds of destruction, even a uniform theory about, or description of, human nature cannot serve as a basis to eliminate evil. Anthropodicy must assume that nature is plastic and subject to basic revision by human effort. In contrast, theodicy begins by assuming that the sources of evil are built into our structure and into human nature. It seeks an answer by asking why creation was structured in this way to begin with. If we carry the sources of our own destruction with us, anthropodicy can report that but it cannot eliminate it. And its basic hope was to do so.

Unless evil can be contained by human revisionist effort, the Gods return. Why? Because religious consciousness opens up again when the awareness dawns on us that we are not in complete control of our own destiny. Anthropodicy purported to put us in control, and when believed it cut off religious sensitivity. It did that for a time for millions who accepted its premises. But the assumptions of the programs of the Social Sciences on which anthropodicy rests no longer look obvious. Few now still hold on to their early optimism to create a science of humanity. This awareness, although it is unconscious for many, has made us increasingly aware of our vulnerability. How could one be sensitive to the presence of the Gods when one assumed that we had usurped the divine power of control and could recreate human nature? The humbling experience of the partial failure of our grandiose schemes for the reform of human nature by the reform of society opens us to the awareness of the presence below of powers from above.

Rudolph Bultman, and others who accepted the modern premise, thought the language of "above" and "below" was too archaic for modern religious use. It is archaic, but it also fits the experience of the human psyche, because the psyche, as Jung pointed out, has archaic origins. When we give our own explanation of evil, we look neither above nor below but to the Natural Sciences. When we become aware of the presence of God, evil is experienced as a falling, a sinking below. Then divine rescue can be experienced as rising above, a lining, an ascent above the normal human plane of psychic life. When evil returns as a religious experience, the language of "above" and "below" becomes meaningful. The Enlightenment taught that the true capacities and powers of human nature were yet to be exhibited in the world. It was not foreseen, however, that one of these capacities is for evil and another is for the destruction of the self and others. Only if all the human capacities we explore can be made entirely good can anthropodicy succeed, because it must explain evil as the fault of a wrong social setting. If, however, in the course of the development of our latent powers, evil is revealed as well as pervasive, anthropodicy fails. Evil stems from our actions, true, but the flaw is latent in our nature and not simply imposed on it. If the individual could change entirely when provided with the right social context, as Marx and all the Enlightenment thought, the story's ending would be quite otherwise. Marx had to attack the theory of natural endowment and "natural rights". The question is not whether all of nature is fixed but whether human nature may be so changed as to eliminate all inherent fault.

Is the self a social creation so that society may change it? Partly, of course, it is. But the question is how far this change can go. Modern Russia is not Czarist Russia, but was evil thereby eliminated? The Marxist wants humanity to end the historical alienation which developed because of the growth of the modern state and its hardening the lines of inequality. But does the rise of the industrialized city give alienation a single external source? If not, alienation returns in new forms in new socio-economic situations reproduced naturally and from within. Becker concludes that it is not enough to play the game of the new society. "Man must confront the underlying alienation that exists in every age" (p. 141). Yet Becker still relies on an anthropodicy. He believes we can find "a commanding view, a unitary critical perspective" which will eliminate alienation. If evil will not fade away on that magic command, or if no such unitary perspective is possible evil re-emerges as demanding an explanation from beyond nature. And the Gods return.

CHAPTER II

LIFE AND DEATH[3]

Fashions shift. One can spend endless time charting these changes and attempting to trace out the causes for them. Occasionally these accidental and capricious shifts--perhaps caused more by our avoidance of boredom than by anything more profound--are significant. Fluctuations in popular fascinations may evidence something deep in the cultural psyche and should not be overlooked. They can be the telltale signs which lead us to a deeper understanding of an age. One such crucial signal from below is the fascination with death and dying. Of course, the failure of the Christian confidence in immortality--even among churchgoers--is one obvious reason for the rise in our insecurity. But beyond that the attraction to the topic of "death" must indicate our confusion over what "life" means.

Surely life and death are correlatives. The understanding of one depends on the other. Any fascination with death tells us that we have become disoriented about the meaning of life. This is understandable in

---

[3]This chapter appeared in an earlier version as an essay in The Journal of Social Philosophy.

America, since many dreams or goals we took for granted have collapsed in recent years. What once we thought to be the aim of our national life no longer seems obvious. Death looms as a special problem when we are not sure what gives life meaning. Corruption, pleasure, travel, gadgets, affluence, technology no longer have an automatic attraction for Americans. Even the goals of democracy and freedom have become questionable.

What does or should life mean, and can we find out how we should live? To live means to create, to enjoy, to give, to worship, to be thankful, to struggle against darkness, and to try to understand. Death, then, means that state where these activities stop or become no longer meaningful. Of course, there are biological and physiological meanings for life and death, as determined by doctors and biologists. It is not the physical meaning of life which confuses us or the death of the body as such which alone causes terror. They are as natural as breathing and not breathing.

Of course, we are perplexed when life is cut short abruptly or when death is unexpected, violent or tortured. Such experiences offer us theological puzzles of a larger dimension. However, our major concern is the obsession over death in any form and our disorientation about how normal life should be lived. Life demands goal-directed action. If our goals are clear, life can proceed and the fear of death need not haunt our sleep out of all proportion. But if we think that life must have one common agreed aim, time brings inevitable challenges to old goals and a demand for new directions. As this happens, we become confused. We feel life no longer has meaning simply because one enduring goal of life has been lost.

One benefit from an obsession with death is that, if the question is turned around, it creates a demand to give life new meaning. If our values and goals are not singular or fixed but move with a certain fluidity and multiplicity, we should expect these shifts to go on constantly, sometimes rapidly, sometimes slowly. We then need to become adept at establishing new values when old ones fade. Of course, some goals remain constant, e.g., freedom and opportunity. It is the flux in minor values in the culture that demands an alertness to discover new approaches. Otherwise meaning in life slips away from us, because we become insensitive to the need for a change in approach.

What can "life" and "death" possibly mean? I have indicated that some of the obsession with death comes from the failure of the Christian conviction about immortality. Can we recover an assurance about a future life? Before we can answer that, we must be sure we know what life and death mean here and now. Of course, these terms may not be exact opposites as at first they appear to be. If they are, "life after death" would be a contradiction in terms. Evidently, "death" means only "to cease to live as one formerly did." This need not exclude "to live in new ways." We use "death" to mean: Withdrawal or a shift away from some one form of life, but this need not mean that other forms are not open. It must be possible to live in several ways and not just in one. Thus, we can "die" in some respects but not necessarily in all. If we do the question becomes: In how many ways is it possible to live, and can we know them all?

To understand death we need to know how many forms of life are available to us. We can die in many ways, that is, cease to live as we formerly did. But can we ever know that we have ceased to live in every possible way, particularly if the forms life can take are infinite? If we cannot exhaust the infinite, we can never be sure death is final. If we experience death in many forms, we must still ask: Can we be sure we have passed beyond every possible form of life?

One attempt to deny death has been to call it a form of life or "a structure of existence," e.g., Heidegger and Jaspers. But to do this is a bit of sophistry. One can experience a moment of death, but it is fleeting. It can never be brought fully into the present as other parts of life can be. If death means the absence of life, it must exclude life in its present form, and all attempts to make death into a part of life fail or are unsatisfactory. One may enjoy friends in the present, or remember one in the past with pleasure. It is impossible that this should happen with death. Death always excludes at least the form of life it terminates.

In Life Against Death[4] Norman O. Brown states that Freud is right, that Modern society is living out a death wish and will succeed in this unless we

---

[4]Wesleyan University Press, Middletown, Conn., 1959.

radically alter our course of behavior. Our present situation is one of a tragic crisis, he believes, which makes us hostile to life. We have no idea what we really want and so we are ready to destroy ourselves. A general neurosis of humankind prevails, which is a psychoanalytic analogue to the theological doctrine of original sin, Brown argues. We are either in flight from, or are alienated by, a reality we find unbearable. Brown's contention supports the assertion that life is connected to death, so that when life becomes disoriented death looms as a problem. Americans once shared a drive to build a "Christian civilization" on this continent, but that aim has faded. With nothing to replace it, we often find ourselves alienated from our national life.

Even this would not be a problem in a Christian context, if we still shared a belief that death can be overcome. The traditional "American Dream" to build a new society on Christian principles was not simply pure primitive Christianity. It was a blend of eighteenth-century utopian theories with schemes of progress. When our immediate religious dreams are thwarted in their fulfillment, this need not mean the end of all religious hope. It is the test of faith to overcome death. This is represented by the disciples' loss of immediate hope in the face of Jesus' death. If we succeed in sustaining faith against loss, a new form of religion is born from the conviction that death has been overcome.

In our time, we experience the failure of some institutional forms of Christianity. Still, death need not loom as a problem if the one who suffers a loss of immediate hope is convinced that this loss of life (i.e., death) can be overcome. If death itself is made the central issue, it is self-defeating since there is no satisfactory way to deal with death on its own terms. New meanings for life must arise. And it does not matter whether this comes in the form of new projects, which substitute for the unrealized Christian civilization on earth, or whether it survives as a conviction that our loss can ultimately be reversed. The classic crisis of Christianity is upon us again: Can the disciple sustain the death of his or her goals and still recover hope?

Perhaps the most profound book on death and modern society is Ernest Becker's The Denial of Death[5]. As a writer, Becker has unusual significance for us because he has a deep understanding and appreciation for both philosophy and theology. He is a sociologist/psychologist who evidences a particular sensitivity to the theoretical foundations of the Social Sciences and the philosophical assumptions on which their theories rest. He is a revisionist who, as we will see, is not himself religious but still has an appreciation of the basis for religion in human nature. Becker opens by quoting Dr. Johnson: "The prospect of death wonderfully concentrates the mind" (p. 12). It certainly seems to be so in our day, but Becker goes on to treat all life as motivated by the fear of death. Life is designed to avoid death by denying it, he thinks. That may be our situation today, and yet it is hard to classify all

---

[5]The Free Press, New York, 1975. All page references are to this edition.

that way. Becker himself still labors under the modern delusion that all knowledge can be summed up with profit for humankind's future plans and that this grand synthesis is just around the corner, if only we will try a little harder. Our central calling is to the heroic, and he thinks modern science is just about to provide the underpinning for a true understanding of the nature of heroism (p. 1). It is hard to see why, after several centuries of trying, Becker still feels science is about to provide this, but that is not the major issue. Becker did write before out disillusionment over the rise of technology as a cure-all had set in.

"The Hero Against Death" could easily be the title of Becker's book. He wants the things we create in society to be of lasting worth and meaning so that they can outlive and outshine death (p. 5). But he feels that the curse of modern society is that "the youth no longer feel heroic in the plan of action their culture has set up" (p. 6). We have become disillusioned over the idea of the noble heroics of whole societies. Optimism in culture was a new form of religion that tried to replace an old faith, but it crumbled as corrupt societies continued to betray this recent human confidence, Soviet Russia being one prime example. In both their ideal and revolutionary models, societies always seem about to deliver us into the promised land. But they never do. The beginnings are enthusiastic; their culminations are less a cause for celebration.

The burden of humanity is appalling, Becker says (p. 51). We have a fear of death but also a fear of life (p. 53). "We don't want to admit that we are fundamentally dishonest about reality, that we do not really control our own lives" (p. 55). Sages have insisted that to see reality one must die and be reborn. But what if "to be born again" means "for the first time to be subjected to the terrifying paradox of the human condition"? (p. 58). "The worry of man's condition is that the deepest need is to be free of the anxiety of death and annihilation; but it is life itself which awakens it, and so we must shrink from being fully alive" (p. 66). If this is true as Becker reports it, it offers us a clue about the decline of vitality in institutional Christianity which once provided an "answer" to this need. Many churches today are either silent or uncertain about immortality and turn their attention to other Christian claims, often social and ethical.

The situation Freud concentrated on has changed, Becker asserts. Because humans are primarily avoiders of death our primary repression is no longer sexuality but death itself. Becker believes psychoanalytic theory could not possibly cure the terror of life and death, so it confronted the problem of sex which it could claim to cure. Thus, we face a disillusionment over Freudian psychiatry as it becomes clear that sex is not our fundamental problem. Freud took the Enlightenment view of immortality, i.e., immortality means being loved by many anonymous people. But as this notion proves unsatisfactory, life and death become our most disturbing problems again. Freud thought humanity could become strong by denying the illusory comforts of religion, but the religious instinct to over come death seems to be winning the battle today. We are moving back to a religious sense of creatureliness after having been briefly the children of science. The terror of death replaces the terror of sex. That is what seems to have happened in our post-Freudian era.

The delusion that scientific power would soon give us control over ourselves and the world made us seem important and vital to the universe, immortal in some way. But the real world is too terrible to admit. If the scientific delusion fades away with the decline in our confidence in technology, the stage is set for a return to religious "illusion", as Freud named it. "Only scapegoats can relieve one of his own stark death fear" (p. 149), Becker says. So we find a plethora of scapegoats offered to us as the source of life's faults. There never will be anything wholly secular about human fear. Humanity's terror is always a "holy terror" (p. 150), which accounts for the religious upsurge as death becomes a preoccupying issue. Since our love object ultimately is God, even the modern all-absorbing concern over love relationships becomes a religious problem and not a wholly natural one. Our public concentration on sex proves to be a disappointing answer to life's riddle.

The problem of modern humanity is the impossibility of getting blood from a stone, of getting spirituality from a physical being (p. 166). We want more from sex than it can possibly give us. When we elevate the love partner to the position of God, we want redemption and nothing less. We expect them to "make us good through love." (p. 167). Needless to say, human partners can't do this. Redemption can only come from outside the individual. Humanity is a theological being not only a biological one, Rank tells us, as quoted by Becker (p. 175). We aren't built to be gods, to take on the whole world. The fear of life and death lies at the base of all human repression, but guilt results from unused life--from "the unlived in us" (p. 180). As modern individuals who sought to escape both guilt and religion we are thrown back upon ourselves in our inability to live life fully, that is to be a hero (Ibid.), Becker explains.

"Man must always imagine and believe in a second reality or a better world than the one that is given him by nature" (p. 188). Our problem is that, in the modern world, we thought this new reality would come to us via the power science released to us. If we have lost that conviction, as many have, our instinct turns us to religious promises again. Like all modern science, psychology promised to usher in an era of the happiness of humanity (p. 190). In fact, what it did was to narrow our range to concentrate on ourselves. Just the thing the neurotic wants to escape. "All the analysis in the world doesn't allow the person to find out who he is and why he is here on earth, why he has to die, and how he can make his life a triumph" (p. 193). Once God was in eclipse, the therapist had to find a replacement or court disillusionment.

The classic sinner and the modern neurotic both experience the naturalness of human insufficiency, except that the neurotic is stripped of the symbolic world-view of God. "The neurotic type suffers from a consciousness of sin just as much as did his religious ancestor, without believing in the conception of sin," Rank reports, again quoted by Becker (p. 197-198). The characteristic of the modern mind is the attempt to banish mystery, but religion offers to solve the problem of death which no living individual can solve alone. Religion takes one's very creatureliness, one's insignificance, and makes it into a condition of hope. We are animals who fear death, who seek self-perpetuation and a heroic transcendence of our fate. "Mental illness" is our modern way of talking about people who have lost courage (p. 209) (see Chapter V). "Fear of life leads to excessive fear of death" (p. 210).

"The creative person becomes, then, in art, literature, or religion the mediator of nature's terror and the indicator of a new way to triumph over it" (p. 220), so Becker maintained. Neurotics, on the other hand, have no gift to offer their fellows or themselves. From time immemorial a distinctive human need has been to spiritualize human life, and this need is intensified in a modern age of science and technology. All heroism is related to some hint of "beyond". The question is: What kind? In what cosmology is one going to perform his heroics? Not everything is possible for us. "What is there to choose between religious creatureliness and scientific creatureliness?", asks

Becker (p. 259). He begins his reply by rejecting Norman O. Brown's solution. "To talk about a "new man" whose ego merges wholly with his body is to talk about a subhuman creature, not a superhuman one" (p. 263).

Marx and Marcuse have suggested that the structure of society must be transformed. But Becker replies: "It is not enough to change the structure of society in order to bring a new world into being" (p. 264). The psychology of humanity also has to be changed, because there is a demonism in human affairs that even the greatest and most sweeping revolution cannot undo. And we have witnessed the truth of this in our own time. Amazingly enough, after explaining why the religious instinct has been revived again after the modern age demolished it, Becker himself opts for psychology as a modern religion (p. 271). He has just explained the failure of all great psychological schemes to date and outlined the depth of the problem in humanity, but he still trusts in a "psychology of the future" to succeed where its predecessors have failed.

In the years since Ernest Becker proposed this joining of psychology and religion into a new belief system, little has emerged to indicate that this is a live option. In fact, Becker himself has explained to us why religion refuses to stay within the confines of any psychological scheme and why we yearn for more than a knowledge of ourselves as a natural animal or else go mad in the fear over life and death. Like so many who feel the resurgence of the ancient philosophical world but do not want to see its return, Becker dismisses "the metaphysical aspects of this problem" (p. 276). And all the while he constructs and proposes his new metaphysical outline of the world. Of course, he is right that if we return to the necessity of developing a metaphysical view of the world, this entails the rejection of modern humanity's hope to end uncertainty.

The religious task is upon us with a vengeance, whether we choose to blend it with psychological schemes or not. Not only have life and death become a problem again at the end of a secular age, religion has itself emerged as a problem and just when we thought that "respectable religions" might have the grace to remain quiet and sedate. Indeed they have, institutionally speaking. Yet beneath their ancient foundations, perhaps prompted by the search for the meaning of life and death, a religious quest boils up which ironically verges on death and destruction itself, due to the intensity of the energy which prompts it. Our only hope for salvation is to find a contemporary religious solution to the question of life and death, one which is adequate to control the terror of the present day.

Ernest Becker wanted to substitute a "science of humanity" for conventional religion, although he wanted it to take over, not ignore, religion's task. His hope for this new science was that it would develop our urge to deny mortality and achieve a heroic self-image. To do this " involves creating culturally standardized hero systems and symbols. However, evil haunts Becker's humanistic scheme. Even if we can construct his life in anthropodicy, his account of evil indicates that it originates in human behavior. If we are sufficiently evil we cannot be counted on to eliminate it, even if the means to do so are placed in our hands. Becker, of course, equates the premises of the Enlightenment with science, as many have. In this case, to admit that we cannot rid ourselves of corruptive internal forces is the same as to abandon the goal of founding an ideal society based on science. The issue is, as Becker admits, whether or not there is something in human nature which prevents us from taking control of our destiny and making the world a sane place for our children.[6]

Becker ties life and death together, since striving to over come death leads us into a fantastic struggle which sometimes goes astray and destroys. The trick is to deny death by creating ourselves as heroes so that life obtains meaning while not allowing evil in, he thinks. For him spirituality becomes an expression of the will to live, which has a Nietzschean ring. We must overcome insignificance, but can we find a way to remain alive in eternity? Cultural perpetuity is Becker's answer, but he recognizes that such a goal is threatened unless evil can be controlled (p. 5). Modern humanity sought control of the world, and this worked until we seem to be destroying it again. When this happened our whole world view began to crumble, because it was based on the premise that we could maintain control. Archaic religious rituals

---

[6]In <u>Escape from Evil</u>, Free Press, Macmillan, New York, 1975. All page references are to this edition.

had power because they linked the individual to the mysterious forces in the cosmos. Our everyday human rituals lack that connection now, Becker admits.

We oppress one another, and unless it can be stopped, this will cause the decay of all cultures. The disillusionment of our time is that none of the proposals (Rousseau, Marx, Lenin, Freud, etc.) have led to full human liberation. Inequality seems to have deeper origins than we at first realized. But "man never was free and cannot be free from his own nature. He carries within him the bondage that he need in order to continue to live" (p. 43). Becker concludes: "Men fashion unfreedom as a bribe for self-perpetuation" (p. 51). In any epoch, what people want is a way to transcend their physical fate. If they can find it, life has meaning and death is not a problem. Of course, Becker thinks we no longer have any problem with sin; we have broken the dichotomy of visible versus invisible by simply denying the invisible (p. 88). Possessions now cause guilt which leads us to frantic contrived designs to earn expiation without God. Most of the evil in the world comes from this drive, Becker postulates.

The issue is whether we now have a complete scientific formula about the cause of evil in human affairs, as Becker affirms (p. 91). He claims that evil stems from trying to be other than we are, that is, trying to deny our animal nature. If so, can this be controlled? We want a stature and a destiny that is impossible for an animal to achieve, and all the while we have lost our romantic image of primitive humanity's peaceful nature. Guilt, sacrifice, heroism, and immortality are Becker's key concepts, and all of these have strong religious origins, of course. Horror comes into this situation because horror alone yields peace of mind. After it subsides, it makes us "right with the world." Homo sapiens is an animal who needs the specter of death to open him to love, Becker assets (p. 116), which may explain some of the rise in the level of terror as traditional religions decline in power. We simply have found no secular equivalents for the theological formula of "victim and redemption."

Becker places guilt and the need for redemption ineradicably at the heart of human nature. Traditional religion dealt with this and gave meaning to both life and death. We must either find a secular equivalent or else revive religion and allow the Gods to return. If we cannot, death will become a problem, because life lacks meaning if this ritual cannot be enacted. "Man still gropes for transcendence," Becker admits (p. 119), and he foresees no end to this. Heroic expansiveness, joy and wonder (those symbols of modern man) have an underside: finitude, guilt, and death. Of such stuff religious experience has always been made. Evil is not easy to eliminate because it rests on our intensity to perpetuate ourselves so that evil rises to a crescendo of fury with any decline of religious conviction and its offer of immortality. Now the traditional religious drama of redemption takes a secular form. We must find symbolic devils, and we will drive them into the wilderness--unless we allow the Gods to return.

All secular societies are lies, Becker admits (p. 124), since there is no secular way to resolve the primal mystery of death. From Marx to Rousseau modern utopian social schemes have all promised us victory over evil and death, just as religion had. Ironically, when we lost the religious dimension to our experience, we actually became more desperate and wild--the opposite of what most utopian schemes presupposed as the condition for their success. But Becker explains that this must be so due to our ineradicable fear of death. The study of society becomes the revelation of a lie, not the celebration of our liberation. Becker asks: "Why are all enjoinders to us to take command of our fears, to stand upright, to build a science in society that rejects rational control--why are these so impossibly utopian?" (p. 162-63). Answer: Because built into human nature, beyond our control, is the fear of death and the search for immortality. Central is the question of whether we are born free and only come into bondage with society, in which case we can hope to be set free, or whether "in the state of nature the solitary individual is already unfree, even before he gets to society" (p. 131). Becker concludes that we carry within ourselves the bondage which we need in order to live, that no new society can of itself offer release no matter what its economic or scientific base. Both Marx and Rousseau thought that if you change society in the right way our natural goodness could flower. If that has not happened, evil must lie in the heart of the creature. The best social institutions can do is to keep it blunted. "The paradox is that evil comes from man's urge to heroic victory over evil" (p. 136). Eugene Ionesco remarked: "As long as we are not assured of immortality, we shall never be fulfilled, we shall go on hating each other in spite of our need for love" (as quoted by Becker, Ibid.).

Our basic human nature is not the neutral vessel the utopian reformers hoped it was. They argued: Change the structure of things and a new society will emerge like a splendid phoenix, free from all impurity and evil because evil lies not in our hearts but in the social arrangements that we take for granted. But it is not so. We are fated to consider this earth as a theater for heroism. We must struggle against evil, since it represents death. To be a hero is to triumph over death, to deliver human nature from the evil of the termination of life. Such heroes are honored, not just in the past but always, as Becker shows us. Since he does not himself favor the return of the Gods, Becker laments: "The tragedy of evolution is that it created a limited animal with unlimited horizons" (p. 133). Ironically, we can less easily manage the expanded horizons of the modern world than the smaller world of the Middle Ages which the moderns so despised as too limiting. We see massive tragedies arise out of massive new power, because science does not touch the root of the human deficiency.

The Enlightenment launched a new paganism; it emphasized the enjoyment of earthly life. The revolutionary hero intended to bring an end to injustice and evil once and for all. This was to be accomplished by bringing into being a new utopian society perfect in its purity. "What are we going to improve," Becker asks, "if men work evil out of the impulse to righteousness and goodness?" (p. 155). Psychology and psychiatry offer us only a new self-acceptance. But this is not what we need or want. One cannot generate a self-created hero system unless we go mad in unleashing power beyond our ability to control, e.g., atomic power. Terrorism has come to characterize what was to have been a scientific utopia.

Guilt must be absolved by something beyond oneself. This is the dilemma of humanity: To whom does one turn for expiation? The psychiatric analysts held this role for some time. But they have proved to be poor gods. They did not believe in the power of evil, and so they could not feel the force of their patients' bondage. The heroes of the Communist revolutions served this function for many, from Mao to Marx to Castro. But when the leaders are tinged with destructive evil, our guilt finds no release. Death must be overcome, since life gains meaning when heroes overcome death, but accomplishing this is dependent on being able to give release from evil. The meaning of life is a religious problem and cannot be otherwise for humanity, however, because we live in a time when, for many, "the Gods have disappeared", it is not easy to recover a sense of the presence of a divinity before whom one can gain release.

CHAPTER III

BEYOND ALIENATION?:[7]

A Theory of Education to Overcome
the Existential Crisis

Existentialism is founded on its discovery that alienation is inherent in the human situation. Of course, like every important philosophical term, we do not all agree about what "alienation" means, what its sources are, and whether it can be cured. Basically, "alienation" means a diverting of normal functions, a withdrawing, and an estrangement of affection. As it has been used in existential literature, the term developed finer shades of meaning and more subtle doctrines applied to it. But with Kierkegaard, it is based on his opposition to the Hegelian dialectic. Yet if a dialectic embraces all of nature, as Hegel thought, and includes humanity, estrangement is temporary and may someday be overcome. Is there a movement which unites disparate elements in a historically developing synthesis, as Hegel thought?

---

[7]This chapter appeared in an earlier version as an essay in <u>Contemporary Philosophy</u>.

Keirkegaard stressed the category of the "individual." He claimed that we are led to realize that humanity is alone and this experience causes dread because it engenders a nothingness which cannot be overcome. Our experience of dread indicates that the world and human affairs are not governed by necessity but by freedom and contingency. This theme appears in all existentialist literature and has been the dominant mood for a whole generation. Religiously, alienation is experienced as separation from God; politically, we know it as the rejection of all utopias created by state control; culturally, it represents our disorientation from traditional values and symbols. Ernest Becker[8] feels that education is responsible for this negative experience and that a new moral view of humanity and society can overcome it. He accepts the existential analysis as being true. However, if an educational program is to overcome alienation, the central existential thesis will have to be revised. Existentialism rejects both mass scale sociological explanations and our ability to extricate ourselves from "the human situation" with any finality.

Becker bases his optimism about education's ability to cure alienation on his conviction that "after one hundred and fifty years of groping, we are at last in position to offer what we have always wanted...a unified, universal college curriculum" (p. ix-x). Becker feels sure that this will enable us to

---

[8]In Beyond Alienation, George Braziller, New York, 1967. All page references are to this edition.

solve the basic problem of making human beings adaptable. He is convinced that this is a great historical breakthrough that has taken place in our time. If true, education could cure alienation, since it would eliminate its social cause. He says, "If the science of man has truly been unified in our time, then the problem of education is naturally solved" (p. x-xi). The whole issue revolved around his "if". Unless such an agreed science of humanity has appeared, we are not in any significantly better position. Becker wrote his optimistic prediction in 1967. What has happened in the intervening years to reverse his optimism, and what significance does this have for existentialism and for education?

First, if we examine the current state of the Social Sciences, we find them further than ever from delivering an agreed science of human nature and some would disclaim that as their aim. In the field of education, primary and secondary schools are in disarray and are subject to a wave of criticism both public and private. The humanities are not neglected in colleges and universities, but often they are less popular. Becker based his optimism on mass education and on the advances of technology which, he claimed, would allow us all to gain a humanistic education. He thought each citizen could learn the moral and intellectual perspectives to infuse society with nobler ideas, but these must not be antiquarian. We need more heroes. They must be based on the Social Sciences and must aim to "liberate" us. He sees education as "the great, new, secular, liberating force in the service of man"

(p. 45). Education, of course, has often been assigned such a role. The issue is whether it can do this only for individuals or whether it can accomplish this for masses in such a way that society itself is transformed. Becker is convinced that, if education recovers the ideals of the Enlightenment, it can become "the beacon to lead men out of darkness" (p. 51).

His first premise was that the university must become a major spiritual power, if all this is to take place. But idealism is currently at a low ebb in universities. Why has this happened, and what does this tell us about Becker's goal? He gives us his own answer: "We need a principle that actually forces man to improve, that compels him with a force of science" (p. 58). Becker holds to the ideal of the Enlightenment: to achieve complete freedom with no coercion. Yet he somehow thinks that science will be a compelling spiritual unifier. However, this convergence has not occurred. We also realize that freedom can be destructive of unification. Science has not become a culturally unifying force, and this is a kingpin in Becker's plan. Free people can wrest dignity from tragedy, he says, and his agreement with existentialism is illuminating at this point. Kierkegaard, Sartre, and Camus concur. However, the difference would be that Becker thinks freedom, if infused by science, will produce uniformity. In opposition, existentialism thinks freedom works to isolate the individual from the mass.

In order to be free, you must not allow majority thought or conventional mores to determine your decision. If the source of the decision is individual and not social, the very act of freedom introduces alienation into the society, particularly from those groups who would like to enforce individual conformity. If so, this has profound consequences for education. Becker seeks a synthesis of knowledge which he thinks can occur if the Social Sciences produce a science of humanity that includes art, religion and philosophy. But if such a synthesis is not possible, acquiring knowledge would only increase diversity and thus estrangement, since there is no unifying core. Our ability to make a decision becomes crucial, but this might isolate the individual from the mass rather than integrate us. If human reason is to liberate humanity, Becker says, "it would have to be universal" (p. 63). And that's the issue. The acquiring of knowledge has not proved able to do this, although many still debate the ideal that it should do so.

Religion has not operated as a unifying force except for small groups of believers, and sometimes it has not always been so even within limited congregations. Unless we want to dismiss morality, we must find a secular basis for it. However, the issue is whether there can be one. We must face up to the Rationalist's faith: Reason is the key to the triumph of natural morality. But the Kierkegaardian critique reappears at this point: Is reason sufficient to determine action, and can it lead us to one conclusion whether implemented or not? Kierkegaard didn't think so and he also thought that reason itself was the partial cause of our indecision. This is because, of itself, it cannot produce a unitary result. Rationalism is a Gnosticism. "A billion ordinary intellects must liberate man" (p. 78). But how has our trust in such a source of liberation turned out? We need to reach agreement on a theory of humanity in society before we can begin to change that society. Yet, if such agreement is not possible, we are pushed back to individual decision and its alienating consequences.

Becker admits that our ability to fulfill the promise of creating "a moral society of free people" depends on the premise that we are basically good if only we can shape a society to serve us. To think that we can do this is an enormous assumption, of course, since most existentialists locate the flow in humanity itself and not in society. Evil for Becker is merely the flaw in the game of society. He is sure that it does not stem from any basic inequity in humanity (p. 145). By contrast, all existentialists treat humanity as isolated and find its flaws as well as its grandeur in itself, all of which we will carry into any society. If so, education may help the individual, but it will never deliver the power to transform society, because the meaning we seek lies on the individual level and not on the social. Becker counts on reason to give us full possession of ourselves. However for existentialism, reason is often the villain. It induces conformity; it stifles action just as much as it encourages it. Perhaps, then, the springs of action lie outside reason.

Freud, of course, argued that the origin of humanity's crippling tendencies lies within. He thought evil was the result of carrying the heavy weight of authority and tradition. A still popular view is one that we must learn not to be afraid to create unique meanings for ourselves. Freud and others thought they could release us from external authority. The early training of the child was the source of evil in the social realm, Freudians claimed, which explains why they counted so heavily on education to eliminate evil. We could create the new society by offering an education free of social restriction.

Our basic problem was the individual's fear to assume the burden of responsibility for providing meaning in his or her own life. The lack of such self-reliance, such autonomy is what causes us to break down. Weakness causes evil. At this point, existentialism and the Enlightenment come close together in theory, but their essential difference lies in the role of education. Becker counts on an agreed new educational program, guided by a new unified science, to change the masses of humans significantly. Existentialism, by way of contrast, sees this as an individual problem which must be solved individually.

Becker is ready to celebrate the fact that, in a relatively short space of time, humanity has "understood the riddle of his own nature" (p. 168). At this point his opposition to existentialism is striking. One may understand; one may decide; one may act. But this is not the same as to say that the riddle of humanity is "solved," they would contend. In fact, existentialism calls on us to be decisive just because the "absurd", to use Camus' term, cannot be eliminated. Thus if education could explain the riddle and make us clear to ourselves our situation would be quite different. But if education cannot be definitive, it may have a function but it cannot transform societies. According to Becker, we have the possibility to achieve a unique kind of freedom. Existentialists talk about freedom too but more as a burden than as a state which offers us release from all restrictions.

It makes all the difference in the world, then, whether or not one approaches education as Becker and the Enlightenment do. They think that human nature can be fully understood scientifically and that this knowledge will free us from evil. This is a modern Gnosticism based on science. On the other hand, if self-understanding is primarily an individual quest, for which all formal education merely provides the data, and if we never attain final knowledge, education cannot be counted on to provide mass liberation and to create new societies. It may provide insight but not radical change. Education may heighten our sensitivities and point out the dilemmas and choices to which we are born, but decision and choice remain lonely burdens which can never be widely shared. To think otherwise is to deceive ourselves. In opposition, Becker thinks we can become a new kind of organism (p. 173). Existentialism disagrees: there can only be contemporary solutions to enduring primal human situations, never final resolutions.

Becker eventually gave up his belief in social utopias. "We cannot engineer a total society according to a drawing board plan" (p. 197). But if he did, how can he still propose to transform us so as to eliminate evil? "By presenting a New Moral View of the World and using it as the basis of instruction in our universities" (p. 198), he replies. Of course, this is only indoctrination unless all first agree on this "new moral view" of the world. But what gives us any right to think this will happen, or that moral opinion will ever be a subject on which all unite?

Psychoanalysis cannot liberate large masses. Becker and others have abandoned that hope. Becker reintroduces a new concept of God in the hope that his will unify us on a plane above the natural, but the history of religion tells us that theology is the last source to which we should turn to find social unity. New proposals to unify ironically turn out to be a source of division. Becker allots to education the task of giving us the vision of the awesome, that is, the new divine mystery. But is it likely that we will get agreement to let mass education inculcate even these vague religious values?

For Becker, a theory of alienation should point out "those evils which could be ameliorated by human effort" (p. 228). In this sense alienation is allied to anthropodicy and can be overcome by the liberation of responsible human powers. Society has conspired to construct human choice; education will liberate it. Becker is thus convinced that alienation will be removed as human choice is exercised. But the existential question is: What if our failure to choose lies within ourselves? And what if, even when it is exercised, the very act of choice itself sets us apart? Choice cannot reconcile us with social norms without contradicting freedom. Choice itself is one source of our continual alienation.

If so, education might inform us but it could not overcome alienation. Human values remain too diverse ever to include all of society in any genuinely individual decision. Becker disagrees: "It would not be difficult to get agreement among men of good will on the theoretical principles of alienation," he claims (p. 239). Becker says this because he still believes the mass will put aside their differences and draw together to improve their lives. But where is the evidence that we can achieve such universal cooperation? If in fact this has not happened, we should suspect that some basic premise in Becker's Enlightenment view is at fault. "On my life, we have it now, or we will never have it" (p. 238), he claims. But his very need to assert this should make us suspect that we may never have it and that we should plan accordingly.

Is this why the writings of the existentialists are so devoid of grand new schemes of education? If you do not believe we can be transformed by any new view of education, it is only marginally useful to keep proposing new educational schemes. Education has a role, an important one, but it is no key to utopia or human release. Our problems are neither that solvable nor that fixed. They are not because, in spite of what Becker thinks, the origin of our problems are not exterior and social but interior.

Becker still believes that the Enlightenment visionaries are correct, even if history has not turned out as they predicted. Of course, his belief is tied to the idea of progress; his conviction is that the progressive liberation of human energies is the road to revolution. By way of opposition, Existentialism is based on the realization that we do not progress as far as our essential situation is concerned. Becker does admit that we have not yet progressed but he attributes this to the fact that "we have not consciously tried to realize a rational ideal of man in society" (p. 253). But is that true? Of course, behind this statement lies his assumption that there is such a thing or that, even if it were produced, it would unify us rather than divide. What is "The Great Truth" for Becker? "Man is good; but society renders him evil" (p. 254). From this Becker proposes to build a whole curriculum. But what if his promise is not correct? In the first place, we will argue about its truth rather than unite around it. If we could unite, education would have a different task.

On Becker's view, evil is the result of weakness, and it can be overcome by breaking our current cultural molds. We have pursued this goal, and evil does not seem to have vanished, all the while our sense of alienation has increased. Alienation stems from our fear of trusting self-reliance, Becker claims. If this is the case, all we need is "a new theoretical ordering of knowledge, with man as center" (p. 280). Isn't this what has been criticized as "the culture of narcissism"? Becker's chief goal lies in the value of the individual persona and the fullest expression of responsible freedom. However, such a philosophy has dominated much of education, and yet our society and our education systems are widely mistrusted and still embroiled in controversy. Research and training are forced to the periphery and self-exploration lies at the center. Modern education often has not felt obliged to teach an inherited body of knowledge or a cultural tradition, because its whole effort rests on this vision to transform human nature.

If existentialism gives a different account of alienation, its source and its cure, what role could it project for education? And does this offer us any insight into our educational confusion? In the first place, existentialism's theory of education differs from Marx, from the Enlightenment, from all theories of progress, and from any social utopian dream. Since the corruption of humanity springs from within, social forces will vary. They provide no uniform cure for our alienation. Thus, education means to increase our awareness as to where the centers of difficulty lie, where our power can be effective, and where individual decision is necessary for control. Education is always involved with Kierkegaard's "subjective" and "objective" problem. That is, all that education offers by way of instruction lies on the objective level. This fact is not unimportant; it sets the issues for us. However, human decision and meaning lie on the subjective level, that is, in the relationship of the individual to what he or she learns and how to act on this.

If education is effective, it should teach us this distinction and not blur it. But all education must begin by admitting that objective learning does not solve the subjective problem of decision. It can inform us that we must not expect a parallel increase in subjective significance simply because there is an objective advance in knowledge. Thus, existentialism need not deny all notions of progress. Mathematics today in Cambridge is different from Plato's time in Athens. But all this tells us is that an advance in objective understanding does not necessarily lead to progress on the subjective level. The two spheres lack a necessary relationship. Our failure to realize this is the source of much of our disillusionment over educational goals, once we achieve them objectively. The individual always remains a problem subject to no uniform solution.

What can we do about alienation, then, since that has been the focus of much contemporary complaint and is the key issue where education is concerned. Can any educational system, existential or otherwise, claim to remove the sources of human alienation? In the first place, the confrontation of our subjective problem with our advance on the objective level tells us that there cannot be a uniform solution such as the nineteenth century hoped for. Solutions are necessarily individual and unpredictable, because alienation results primarily from the discrepancy between a solution on the objective and the subjective plane. Tension is necessarily created as knowledge advances, so that alienation must be experienced before it can be overcome. More social change cannot cause alienation to disappear. This is not to say that any given change proposed for society may not be good as an objective plan and that some social conditions are bad if they go uncorrected. But it does say that human alienation and its cure do not begin on the social level.

This explains our personal disillusionment over the social changes we have achieved and the lack of satisfaction on the human level we often feel about our objective accomplishments. We constantly expect such improvements to relieve our anxiety with finality, but they do not do so. Existential education can prepare us for that result, although it must be experienced before it can be felt as true. No educational scheme should ever offer to remove alienation once and for all, since we know alienation to be innate. Any theory which proposes its removal is a theory of "idealism" that is out of touch with human reality. We may continue to think we can remake the world and humanity along the lines of our ideal. Existential education knows that, beautiful as its creations can be, rational thought can also be devious and destructive unless it admits that life lived is never the same as life thought.

CHAPTER IV

THE METAPHYSICS OF PSYCHOLOGY[9]

In separating itself from philosophy, psychology hoped to avoid metaphysics by becoming a science. Due to its history within the life of philosophy, psychology understood only too well that all theories about the psyche had been based on the assumptions of some philosophical view. Plato saw the soul in one way, Aristotle in another. Now, using the tools of Modern Science, would it be possible to build a psychology that depended on no philosophical assumptions? If so, psychologists could hope for the universal acceptance which had always eluded philosophers. They might achieve this if the subject matter of psychology were just like the subject matter of the physical sciences, or if the application of common methodology were in itself sufficient to render results universal.

The basic assumptions of any era hardly seem like assumptions at the time but more like truths. In addition, the conceit of the moderns was to

---

[9]This chapter appeared in an earlier version as an essay in the International Philosophical Quarterly, Vol. XXII, No. 1, Issue No. 85, March 1982, pp. 35-41.

think that at last we stand face to face with truth. Today we realize how many assumptions were involved in the project to build a scientific psychology. Like most assumptions that stem from an earlier age, we realize that now we share few of them. One is that if psychology is to escape philosophy, it must be possible to build a universally accepted psychological theory. But we do not see this happening. In addition, few think it desirable. An age of pluralism in theory always becomes a metaphysical age. "Metaphysics" does not only solve differences; it means the comparison of first principles one to another.

Another more important assumption concerns psychology; can it be accounted for by uniform laws? A third assumption of determinism is usually involved, since freedom of the will, contingency, and indeterminism make the formation of laws impossible in psychology. Furthermore, a fourth assumption about non-transcendence of a nature exists. But if we live on more than one plane of existence, some crucial portion of our psyche will elude the observer. All these notions, or course, are part of what we call "the modern temper." As long as these assumptions were believed to be truths, psychology was safe from philosophical vagary. But secretly and quietly our confidence in first principles of the modern age have been eroding. That leaves these assumptions as only one set of first principles among many, all of which must be compared and evaluated. A "metaphysical age" is one that is unsure of its first principles and is constantly involved in self-questioning.

Unfortunately, psychology as a pure science does not fare well in an age of uncertainty.

The modern temper, along with Freud, wanted to trace all human crippling to early indoctrination and trauma induced by parents or society. To do so makes the psyche manageable. If the self takes root in a society and family, we can track its origins. But if the self is open to experience worlds other than the natural, our psychology must take a quite different form. A theory of personality as the result of genetic development, such as Freud offered, is perfect to use as a scientific base. But if it excludes all aspects of human experience, or if it fails to cure us, his theory of psychology suffers. Freudianism is itself an anthropodicy, that is, a human account of the origin of evil. It gives us a theory of the alienation of humanity in society and outlines the path to achieve a cure. Our problem is: What happens when multiple theories become acceptable? What happens if we reject the thesis of anthropodicy?

The meaning of human "will" is the crucial concept, of course. Is it no more than "internalized social values"? If it is an individualized non-viewable center of decision, capable of acting outside the determining physiological forces which surround it, psychology as a science fails. We may of course assume that "will" means something simpler to assimilate it to scientific theories, but what other than our wish fulfillment guarantees us that this is so? If humanity behaved like a rat we would be more predictable, but which premise makes the most sense of the grandeur and the chaos of human history, Freud or, say, Plato? Of course, one theory is that our past history will come to an end and we will then be able to transform the future. That is an alluring dream, but what evidence is there that it will come true? Science has changed must of the external aspects of existence, but has our inner life been similarly altered? We may assume a principle which states that "the outer shapes the inner," but is this more than simply one principle among many?

Ernest Becker wants "individual subjectivity, as the creator of values," to occupy the center of a new science (p. 158)[10]. If we allow subjectivity into our account of human nature again, can the end result be a "science" in any recognizable sense? An Enlightenment science, Becker adds, "must be a science in which human control is possible. Otherwise it is simply not a science" (pp. 160-61). But what if human control is at best partial and never fully possible? The Enlightenment did not argue out its metaphysical assumptions on this point, but then all new assumptions become manifest later rather than in their own time. If it were not so, we would never move forward but would only argue various premises. If we enlarge the meaning of "science" to include poetic, artistic and religious meanings, as Becker suggests (p. 168), do we have a science in any sense that does not stretch the

---

[10]Ernest Becker, The Structure of Evil, The Free Press, New York, Macmillan Publishing Co., Inc., 1968. All page references are to this edition.

term beyond its meaning? Do we really create our own meanings or are they on the whole given to us from outside ourselves?

Ernest Becker provides his own answer to the dilemma of the early restrictiveness of the principles behind modern psychology. He wants us to create our own meaning in poetry and art, to give ourselves immortality in an aesthetic object. There is nothing wrong with this. Aesthetic achievement has been a religious substitute before, but it is a theory which fits special persons, not the ordinary ones. Such creativity is an achievement for the rare individual, not the many. It is so far from being an obvious solution that only a few could accept it. The aesthetic world would suddenly become the locus of all significance and bear the burden which the religious life formerly had, that is, to give meaning to life.

Becker sees that humans have a need for a religion, but he thinks this can be manufactured by the "full and creative use of our symbolic, imaginative equipment" (p. 199). Becker also recognizes that, if we create our own meanings, they perforce have no higher authority and so we may distrust them as our means of "salvation". We must invest something with ultimate meaning, but can aesthetics serve this function? Without god, we force human creations to assume this burden. We may claim we create force but it is a hard task when we must hold up the world alone. To overcome the accompanying sense of desperation, we must believe in our own overriding value. This returns us to anthropodicy again; that is, we account for evil as man-made. We can sustain such a belief only if we think we have a way to eliminate evil from human experience. Thus, the re-emergence of evil as cataclysmic destruction shakes the foundations of the humanistic attempt to create dignity. If we have only the artistic world to sustain us, it must be supported at all costs. Even though evil's continued presence in the world calls into question our ability to build an authentic world on our own power.

If, as Becker suggests, "every man must be his own artist, his own creator of convincing meaning" (p. 210), we have come a long way from psychology as a social science and are very close to philosophy as a constructor of various world views. Only a few people have artistic genius. Most will find their meaning elsewhere, which opens religion as an alternative. Of course, a common reply is: But Becker is not representative of psychology today and is a strange thinker. The issue lies deeper. Has he put his finger on the deficiency in psychology as a human science? Are we driven to some human construction of meaning such as he offers if we want to understand the human psyche.

Becker wants psychology to "show why human conduct assumes particular forms in each epoch" (p. 211). He thinks this can be done by documenting the constrictions which a whole range of social institutions place on us. But this is philosophy more than a science of psychology. First, you have the question of whether this can or should be done on a mass basis.

More important, the first principle Becker assumes is that conduct is determined by physical causes, actually restricted by social institutions, and that all conduct varies with the epoch according to general laws. These are enormous assumptions, even if they are widely accepted in an age of historical study. However, it may be true that eras and social institutions explain only the detail, like differences in dress and custom. Whereas, if conduct is individually determined, no universal laws or explanation may be possible. If this is so, psychology as a science must be reexamined. Perhaps the principle that institutions and eras determine conduct is accepted because it fits a certain theory we want to be true, rather than because the facts prove it.

Becker thinks "modern man" has "lost the possibility of the intensive creation of life meaning" (p. 213) and that this is our problem. Again, this is more philosophy than empirical psychology, because: Who established that it is possible for us to "create" meaning rather than find it. Is meaning constructed or is it given to us? Humanity is a meaning creating animal, Becker tells us, but he has defined humanity so as to make this true. Becker vaunts the Middle Ages, because he thinks they established aesthetic meaning socially. Is that the way the Middle Ages would have seen itself, or would they insist that meaning was religiously given? Following Comte, Becker wants to create a secularized version of the Middle Ages which will "promote the worship of humanity, based on love, dedicated to ideals and progress" (p.

223). But can we manufacture such religious zeal without God?

Is history really the record of "the flowering of the human personality" (p. 226), or is that a romantic illusion and conceit? What is "history" is a central and unresolved question. Becker paints a picture of a future society which has all the zeal and altruism of medieval monasticism. Isn't this more philosophical speculation than a description of how society is or is likely to develop? Even if we could agree on Becker's ideal of each of us being our own artist, do we have any reason to believe that more than a handful of individuals are ever strong enough to create meaning in their own lives? Becker wants ritual and celebration to heighten life. Can one celebrate his own achievements, or does the significance of a ritual arise and tie us to a sphere beyond the human? Becker admits that modern life often seems bankrupt and hollow. But he does not want to settle for an existential absurd.

Man has the burden of creating his own meaning, Becker tells us. We must reach for the meaning which transcends us. This is a possible philosophical view. In saying this Becker is not a typical social scientist; he has turned secular evangelist. The question is whether he is right, that the Social Sciences must either give up their original schemes of reform or reach back to philosophy to create the world view needed to add the dignity they seek. Psychology must help the artist provide meaning, according to Becker, but the very task and function of psychology is the issue. If there is not an agreed function for psychology, we are back to philosophy and the comparative study of basic postulates. Becker says humanity is free "when he enjoys a rich participation in a broad panorama of life experiences" (p. 247). This may be true, but surely such a statement is more a philosophical definition than a product of Social Science research.

"Every man his own genius." This seems to be Becker's proposal as our only way out after the rejection of philosophy. He is explicit about the need for the reintroduction of theology, although it is now to be a self-creation of man. We must validate our meanings without the assurance of God. But can we, or at least can more than a few individuals do so? Becker wants us to find absolute value, absolute meaning in nature. Yet for centuries philosophers have been arguing over whether that is possible. Becker says that "competitive egoism" is not natural (p. 262), but certainly that is a philosophical postulate not a simple fact. If so, the hope to build religious altruism without God fails. Becker wants human association to take the place of a worship of the divine. What leads him to think this will be any more than destructive competitiveness? Becker thinks we have created "mass humanity" because we have denied free and spontaneous life (p. 279). Only a romantic philosophy could assume that freedom and spontaneity automatically produce the good life for all.

However, you protest that you do not like Becker's view of what humanity should become. You hold to a different meaning for psychology, you say. My point is still that there is no neutral, final, universal definition of "humanity," but only a series of philosophical postulates any one of which may for a time seem obvious and final to a certain group. For instance: "Man becomes truly man by the aesthetic transformation of the world with his free directive energies," Becker tells us. That is a grandiose postulate, not a description of us as we are. He says the failure of our time is "the failure of the science of man to put forth an agreed, synthetic theory of human nature" (p. 281). The key term here is "agreed." Even if we agree that there is any such thing as a "synthetic theory of man", nothing in our past suggests that we will ever unite on one definition of man. We get such a definition only on the basis of philosophical assumptions (e.g., one based on "aesthetic transformation"), and philosophy is always controversial.

Freedom and genius are the educational goals Becker postulates. Like the Enlightenment, Becker puts an enormous burden on education. He in fact counts on it to produce the new utopian society. What evidence have we that education can produce such massive change? Education should be aimed not at the existing world but to create an ideal world, you say. Can we agree on what that world should be? Becker sets a high goal for what he calls "progressive education" (p. 293). Of necessity, this will be education for the few not the whole of society. If so, society may be improved but never totally remade. Without questioning it, Becker accepts "individualism" as the great goal, but we do not all accept that. He says that "without a unitary, critical world view human dignity and social order are impossible" (p. 307).

But if we have little evidence that we <u>all</u> will unite on this, the utopian vision remains unachievable, since it depends on united action.

Auguste Comte wanted metaphysical philosophy to disappear, Social Science to be created, and positive philosophy to be founded. John Dewey thought that if only philosophers studied humanity as an organism in society this would result in a synthesis of science with education, morals, and religion. Since this has not happened, we may be dealing with a metaphysical postulate which Dewey simply assumed and not with a postulate of science. Becker admits:

> The idea behind the fervent hope of a science of man was to put the world firmly into the hands of its most advanced creature. The quest for the unity of knowledge, for the merger of science and philosophy, was a quest for an agreed basis on which men could act and shape the world into something less unhappy, less evil. (p. 310).

The assumptions involved here are enormous: That we can all agree, that the natural order is itself a source of human hope, and the we can be trusted when put in charge. Evil must be either illusory or in our power to overcome. If these postulates are either not accepted or are not true, the project fails.

Becker is looking for the single unifying principle that will form an integrated science (p. 327). Is there one? He offers a universal principle for human action which he says is akin to gravitation in the Physical Sciences. Can this be found? He calls it "self-esteem maintenance." Is that on a par with the laws governing gravity, or is it more like a philosophical postulate? He is convinced that the twentieth century has solved the problem of the unity of the science of humanity (p. 339) and all disciplines can join around a single focus. If this has not happened, as seems to be the case, our suspicion is that we do not have one focus but many. Evil can be overcome, Becker postulates (p. 346), and in that way the problem left to us by the decline of medieval cosmology can be solved. But if the problem is "solved," as Becker claims, and yet our life remains unchanged, we need to check the adequacy of our philosophy not our science.

"How do we finally establish a synthetic science of man?", Becker asks (p. 360). And he answers: By agreeing on the rationally compelling nature of the new anthropodicy, that is, a naturalist theory of what makes people act the way they do and why they are unhappy. That sounds good, but the catch lies in his little phrase, "by agreeing." He knows that this is difficult; somehow he thinks the problems are the same for a science of humanity as for the physical and natural sciences. However, a brief glance at the current state of affairs in the sciences hardly warrants such optimism. One must have faith in our potential to increase ethical action. That is a faith hardly warranted by the facts any more than faith in God's existence. We must make a "willful option that is at all times based on incomplete knowledge," Becker admits (p. 366). That sounds more like William James' argument for the "will to believe" than the program for a science. And even if it were, unity certainly is the last thing it will bring about, since we know that even the medieval church could not be held together except by force.

The Enlightenment which sought to eliminate religion and faith offered itself as a science. But where humanity is concerned we return to the admission of our inability to reshape humanity or society on the basis of pure science alone. Becker wants all social scientists to work toward a projected vision of the good life which the whole society will work toward in unison (p. 368). If there is no evidence all will do this, there must be something questionable about the postulates involved. For instance, perhaps values are not unified and actually work so as to divide people. If so, there is no single vision of the good life we can ever expect all people to share.

Becker was aware that if this is all to happen, fact and value must be fused. Are "fact" and "value" such that this is possible? He admits that accomplishing the vision of a new humanity depends on our ability to "banish evil in the social realm" (p. 369). That is a startling phrase, is it not, since evil has not fled from the human scene. He wants an "increasing development of human purpose," but that is based on the romantic premise that we human beings are naturally good, for which there is little evidence. The whole project stands or falls on whether we can eliminate evil by human action, which Freud and Marx and Comte believed. Becker is candid enough to admit that "we cannot tolerate any theoretical approaches to man which take a dim view of human nature" (Ibid.). Considered scientifically, isn't a dim view of human nature more realistic than Becker's romantic vision of excluding all evil?

Becker indicates that much of the early enthusiasm of the Social Sciences rests on a romanticism about human nature and trusts the unlimited nature of human development. Our early Puritan preachers were far less visionary and idealistic than this. Becker's proposal to renew his vision comes precisely at a time when our disillusionment over our ability to carry out utopian schemes without spoiling them is at its depth. Becker assumes that our knowledge of humanity will increase and provide us with a means to control it. Force and coercion have always been with us, but what evidence can we give that psychology will produce anything to give us a means of control? Becker again wants us to trust humanity as the Enlightenment did, but isn't it part of our present dilemma that we have done that?

Becker admits that the whole Enlightenment tradition is at stake. He also says that "for the science of man, evil must be somehow amenable to human control" (p. 379). Isn't that precisely where the Enlightenment dream founders? We can postulate a program in which evil is placed within human control, but we must critically evaluate such an assumption against others, since the world we live in gives little evidence it can or will change fundamentally. We can, of course, retreat and make no such grand claim as his goals for Social Science. Becker agrees with Dewey that "the rise of modern experimental science meant that man set out to discover the world and place it under his control" (p. 390). If we surrender this, we have changed the science of humanity radically from the goals of a Natural Science. We can do this, but it involves a tacit admission that there is something about human nature which defies scientific control.

Becker tells us that "we must place the highest priority on those values which permit free and creative human action" (p. 395). In the first place, we have no agreement on what "free" and "creative" mean. That which began with the aim to avoid philosophy either returns to it and to the controversy and uncertainty which surrounds it, or else it must abandon its projected task to create a science of humanity. The whole project stumbles on the notion of an anthropodicy. If evil cannot be accounted for on a wholly human plane, and cannot be eliminated by us, our program to remake ourselves cannot be advanced in the way we remake nature has. Humanity remains our problem.

CHAPTER V

SALVATION AS A RETURN TO MENTAL HEALTH[11]

A.   The Modern Hope to Replace Salvation with a New Science

When we think of "mental health," we have not recently connected this to the notion of "salvation" as outlined in Christian doctrine.   There once was a time, of course, when many who wanted to recover or restore mental health turned to Christianity and some found their healing.   There are, I suppose, many reasons which can be given for why this ceased to be true, but at least one of these involves the rise of psychiatry as a profession and the well-known anti-religious sentiments of its pioneers, most notably Sigmund Freud.   Psychiatry arose as the modern and "scientific" alternative to the healing and counseling practices of Christianity, which of course had often failed to cure.   Before we can decide whether "salvation" can once more be seen as one road to mental health, we must consider how psychiatry came to replace it.

Ernest Becker is a good guide to assist us in this reappraisal.   He is a

---

[11]This chapter appeared in an earlier version as an essay in <u>Faith and Reason</u> and was presented as a paper at an International Religious Studies Conference meeting in Wellington, New Zealand, August 22-25, 1983.

champion of the scientific status of the Social Sciences, and he believes in their ability to revolutionize the study of humanity. He has written about the role psychiatry played in this venture[12] and he is an astute critic of psychiatry. At the same time he is a supporter of its claim to supplant traditional religion. The subtitle of his book is "The New Understanding of Man" and it considers whether a superior and perhaps scientific knowledge of humanity became available which outdated all previous religious proposals for the healing of the spirit. Should all "mental illness" now be defined as coming under the general category of "the science of humanity"? If so, mental health can no longer fall within the province of religion.

Briefly put, Becker's book massively documents the failure of the Social Sciences to achieve their proposed revolution in the understanding of humanity such that psychiatry becomes another area of science. He traces the reason for this failure to the founding assumptions of the Social Sciences. Still, he remains optimistic; all we need to complete the proposed revolution is a reordering of those original assumptions. As Becker sees it, the chief problem is that "disciplinary proliferation" has had the effect of burying humanity. Thus, the Social Sciences have failed to give us the clear, whole perspective on humanity we need in order to cure our ills. To accomplish this Becker proposes a "radical recentering of the human sciences" which would take humanity's self-value as "the proper invariant point of reference

---

[12]<u>Revolution in Psychiatry</u>, The Free Press, New York, 1964.

79

around which the various disciplines should revolve their efforts" (p. ix). In other words, Becker thinks that our failure does not lie in the original assumption which launched the Social Sciences but in a methodological problem. Having failed to date, we can still proceed to build "a mature hypothetico-deductive science" (p. x), or so Becker is convinced.

Of course, others have proposed that we adopt this "human-centered" orientation. What is new in Becker's proposal is that he believes we now have enough knowledge to forge a broadly inclusive and logically consistent science of humanity. Becker admits that we have lived through an era of "disciplinary morass." Nevertheless, for reasons which are not quite clear, he thinks it possible to transform this into a "compelling rational basis for moral action" (p. x). Most Social Sciences began with a crusading goal of this kind. They wanted to improve the lot of humankind, but their zeal was lost somewhere along the way as disciplinary cross-fire developed between them. The goal Becker sets out for us is to overthrow the "narrow medical view of human ills" (p. 2). Psychology, he thinks, must merge into a broad human science. "Mental illness" is cultural behavior and not simply a narrow medical phenomenon.

Part of Becker's rejection of the role of traditional religion in mental health stems from his conviction that the Enlightenment has come, making all things new. "Man has on the whole become more sophisticated and rational" (p. 59), he asserts. If this is true, new techniques are demanded and old ones are automatically outmoded. Becker admits that humanity's need is "to forgive himself each night, to absolve himself so that he can begin again, anew" (p. 70). This is the classical religious notion of confession and forgiveness, but Becker feels that today "religious motives have little to do with life as most people live it" (Ibid.). If true, religion can be of no assistance in performing this needed task. The appearance of schizophrenia "sums up man's coming of age in society" (p. 108). In other words, rather than decreasing psychic illness, evolutionary advance increases it as we shed our need of religion and stand alone.

Action breaks down when the individual's sense of self-value is undermined. If we live in a secular world without appeal, we must create a symbolic worth on our own, Becker urges. "When the individual does not control meanings symbolically, we call him "mentally ill"" (p. 120). Although we have been at odds about all this for 50 years, Becker for some reason thought (in 1964) that happily "the data of the human sciences are starting to emerge; their relationships are becoming clear" (p. 132). Whether or not his optimism is soundly based is a crucial matter. If the day of religious help is passed, such that our being alone in the modern world actually increases mental illness, then all is lost. That is, all is lost unless the social sciences are about to reach a level of agreement so that they can step in and provide the needed solution. Cultural advance gave us this problem in the first place, according to Becker. "As soon as the theological world view was undermined, humanity was doomed to examine his miserable condition" (p. 138).

This is a neat reversal of the usual charge that religion needlessly places humankind under a burden of guilt from which the Modern Age, at last, can release us. "Man has rolled up his shirt sleeves, eager to tamper with his own creation" (p. 139), but the result is to make us less secure rather than more. On the positive side, Becker is convinced that we are close to developing an ineluctable law for human development. If true, this would help us reverse the tide and restore our lost mental health. To be possible, all depends on his theory that human motivation owes almost nothing to primary biological drives. Thus, if humanity is self-created via his culture, the animal side counts for less. If all our conduct has been learned, it can all be unlearned. We have a very plastic creature on our hands which we can remold, that is, if an agreed law of human development is in our possession as Becker thinks it is. We no longer find it possible to give a purely physical interpretation of humanity. But in spite of the important role this gives to symbolism, Becker thinks it is possible to found a precise science of humanity.

But we must ask Becker: In rejecting the doctrinal rigidity of Freud as he does, have we not also done away with the possibility of finality? If so, are we in the assured position to cure mental illness, which he agrees stems from our loss of the theological world? Becker claims to see the human personality from the inside, and it holds no more mysteries for him. He thinks since the culture we create is a fiction, "the kind of people we make depends upon the kind of people we want" (p. 167). Unlike the notion of original sin, our present restrictions have been caused by artificial restraints over which we can now assume control. We no longer need to struggle against ourselves or against forces deep within our nature. Rather, our only opponent is a world we ourselves have fashioned during our early training.

The anxiety we now face arose from the possibility of abrogating our entire framework of meaning. But as this happened, our world also shed its mystery. We lost a world, but on the other hand we now know how to build a new one. Our neurosis grows due to a failure to symbolize and also by constricting our possibilities of choice. If anxiety arises due to a failure of words that symbolize, this matter is now subject to our control. However, the issue we must face is: Do we really create our world? It would be much easier for us to solve our psychic problems if this were true; Becker is right about that. He thinks we know where to pin the blame for human failure: On the flimsy symbolic basis for human meaning we ourselves constructed. If this is the case, "there is very little about the peculiar human condition that is not somehow in man's potential control" (p. 183). Guilt and shame, though typically human, have been made by us and so may be unmade by us. Yet the issue remains: Do we really create our world at will? If we do create it, of course we can change it.

In his quest for autonomy, modern humanity is forcing culture's hand because, Becker is convinced, we are about to gain control over humanity by learning how to construct culture. All we need to do is liberate ourselves from the fetters of the excessive restraints of our early environment. This formula sounds easy enough, but is it working today? Becker simply assumes that humanity has full control over the means to construct culture. Can we agree to that? He defines "the world" as rational and as self-constructed; therefore it can be reconstructed. "Mental illness" becomes simply our failure to practice "a fully rational approach to interpersonal living" (p. 206), Which Becker assumes we have now learned how to do at will. He adopts a traditional Enlightenment view: It is "ignorance" that accounts for the seemingly irrational behavior of the mentally ill. Thus, our illnesses can be cured by the new knowledge which has recently come into our possession.

Medical psychiatry, of course, can no longer be in charge of the revision of humanity, since accomplishing this change depends on developing a symbolic view of humanity and the world. Becker's account makes mental illness easy, and so it can be cured easily. It only depends on restructuring our world views. Schizophrenia turns out to be a stupidity. The victim is said to lack behavior patterns to manipulate means and ends. Thus, the "normal" individual is now defined as the creative one, "the one who exercised control over his choice of means and ends" (p. 209). The history of modern psychology, thus, becomes a history of its own disillusionment as a science. "Psychology has evolved back into philosophy," he thinks (p. 120).

Becker does not seem aware of his own assumptions; that is, his whole theory seems obvious to him. He has turned psychology into a social philosophy. He thinks we can now stamp out mental illness by putting the control of means and ends sequences back into the hands of the people who need to make the choices. It is just that simple. As he has defined it, we now are faced with the opportunity to control the social world (p. 125). Becker makes this assertion in response to his inquiry into psychoanalysis. We can wrest control of the tools of mental health from religion, but only if we establish a new science which can exercise that kind of power, he thinks. But if the modern world has failed in this effort, Christianity with its less precise doctrines is not in such an unfavorable position.

However, this change in humanity's mental health, which Becker is so sure the Social Sciences can induce, requires all human beings to change together. Since in the past criticism of religion often centered on its piecemeal approach and its lack of ability to change whole cultures, the new Social Science approach is based on mass change. If it is not, we are back to the village priest counseling his parishioner. Psychiatric problems represent human failures, because they indicate a lack of human control in situations where decisive choice is called for. Since our failure is thought to depend on an ignorance of the possibilities present in an ordered world, once we realize this mass change should come by maximizing individual choice, or so Becker postulates. If it is the individual who controls his own choice rather than some "science," you have to be sure the individual will always seek change as he or she is supposed to. Maximizing choice may be the only way to meet the challenge of twentieth century society, but Becker treats it as a matter of "available vocabularies of motivation" over which the individual lacks free control. The "real problem" is the one of "individual integration" (p. 128), he says. But isn't Becker operating under a delusion: That once we instigate a little something new in education, each individual will suddenly take over the task of creating himself or herself and all will be fine. There are powerful interests that wish to curb human spontaneity, such as Marxism. Becker can only carry out his analysis by assuming that what he says is true of every human everywhere, not just of some. Becker says: "We seem to be calling for nothing less than a total reenlistment of society in the furtherance of human design" (p. 225). What is the evidence that all peoples will ever join together for any cause?

At this point what we must ask Becker is: Will altering culture through education really produce free individuals, each one capable of handling decisions, or will this procedure merely inculcate another type of conformity? Becker thinks we face "a total social problem" (p. 228). He has the power, via the new science, to program us for a full exercise of human freedom. "The twentieth century is witnessing a revolution in self-awareness that has not been seen since the Renaissance and the time of the Greeks," Becker asserts some what expansively (Ibid.). However, we need to assess this claim carefully to see if his thesis really can produce the mental health he desires. Like so many others, Becker gives aesthetic experience a particularly heavy role. It takes the place of both religion and God in its healing potential: "The aesthetic object shows that the perfect union of ends and means is possible. It embodies...the vision that fulfillment is possible" (p. 233). Art takes on the same function as the Marxist goal of the classless society or the Christian heaven.

Religious ritual, which has long been used as an avenue to restore psychic balance, is dismissed. Aesthetic ritual takes its place. "This is the function of ritual, to interweave inextricably the symbolic and the organic, by gesture and sound, body balance, measured movements" (p. 237). That is the modern avenue to mental health. But if we ask why art is expected to do so much for us now, we have to reply: Because religion isn't doing it. "The aesthetic object demonstrates that life is not in vain, by holding up tangible proof of human creativity" (p. 239). Art can provide the meaning to life which formerly religion did, and Becker never denies that our mental health demands this kind of guarantee of human significance. Just as religion used to transcend the world, so Becker thinks aesthetics now takes humanity beyond the confines of culture. Human values become supreme.

In a pre-scientific day religion stressed the healing power of love, and now Becker ties love to aesthetics. He sounds like St. Paul writing his letter to the Corinthians when he says: "Thus love banishes shame, transcends the fictitious learning, the sham morality" (p. 241). The primary aim of psychotherapy is accomplished by love, or so he feels. "The individual accepts his past and his uniqueness as irrevocable, as necessarily and desirably so" (p. 240). Since the love object functions as the psychotherapist, we encounter here the counterpart of the religious claim that "Jesus accepts you" or "God loves you." But our question must be: Is this true for all or even for most cases? Is Becker treating love as a romantic ideal rather than as it exists in fact? Love may mirror the religious experience of release that we have all so long found healing, but can love and aesthetics accomplish this alone and for everyone? Perception and contemplation of the unique, existential, loved-object has taken the place of the mass, confession, and forgiveness.

Becker wants the loved object to function as the psychotherapist, or perhaps we should say, as the priest. Jesus accepts you; God loves you. The prime religious experience is that of release. But can art and a love object do this as well? Becker has set us up in a situation which does not eliminate our religious needs but rather makes them irrevocably a part of human nature. Then he goes on to propose that these same functions be shifted to a non-religious office. Becker ties love to beauty so that art becomes central in overcoming the split between self and world. The love object somehow adds the meaning life needs in order to become meaningful. Love now has the power to forgive, a power which we formerly sought in God. Of course, what must be noted again is that this assertion depends on a very idealized notion of "love." In some circumstances love is as much the source of our bondage as of our release.

Recognizing that our situation at the present time is not quite like the picture he paints, Becker puts a great deal of stress on the change education can bring about in the future. If the future is to be different from the past, what will provide this change? Becker places his hope in education. He wrote <u>Revolution in Psychiatry</u> in 1964. What has happened to education in the meantime? Rather than agreeing on a new educational program and then implementing it, we are in even greater disagreement about our educational programs, and many think the whole system is faltering. Rather than freeing us, education itself has become a prime source of controversy. We are surely further from an agreed educational agenda than when Becker wrote. If so, does that offer us much optimism about the likelihood of accomplishing his revolution via education and providing a substitute religion? Becker has defined us into a religious situation of need, but has he left us any way to satisfy this short of a return to tradition?

In a later book (1969) Becker again stresses his aim to "educate, elevate, and free man" (p. vii).[13] The problem with this, of course, is that

---

[13]<u>Angel in Armor</u>, The Free Press, New York, 1969. All page references are to this edition.

such a change must be achieved universally; it cannot be accomplished by giving an elite education to a few. Traditional religion has been criticized because it offered release only to its few devoted followers. The aim of the Modern World was to universalize this process, to open release to all humankind. To realize this goal Becker pinned his hope on a new understanding of humanity and on an educational program which is scientifically based, just as Marx pinned his hope on an economic theory and social revolution. But the hoped for universal agreement on a new theory of human nature has not materialized, all the while our trust in education as a tool to release us has been disappointed time and time again.

We need, says Becker, "a rich and meaningful world" to which we can be committed (p. 10). But even if this is the case, the issue is: Can we create this process for ourselves and keep it under our own control? To put it simply, Becker proposes a new alternative to the Christian offer of salvation. His is based on the same perception of our human need, but he takes the power from God's hands and places it in humanity's. Our problem might be so different if Becker did not assert that all men and women do need release, forgiveness, and restoration. Like Camus' The Fall, he has placed us in a situation of religious need but offers a secular solution. We must assess the basis of Becker's optimism and decide whether something new has been added so that it now enables us to be optimistic about self-rescue when we could not be before. There is no question but that psychiatry deals effectively with some special cases, but can it cure "the human predicament"?

The proposed program of the Social Sciences and modern psychiatry has existed long enough so that, even if we do not pronounce it a total failure (which would be too harsh), we can say that it has not had the universal releasing effect its enthusiasts hoped for (which is also true of Marxism). To some eyes, the rise of modern science made religion's promise of cure obsolete, but Becker's reappraisal of the Social Science program actually makes religion a viable option again. If a final secular cure has not appeared as the modern alternative we hoped for, no alternate source for our mental health can be ruled out as antiquated. If we reject the long-assumed notion that we now live in a day of an absolute line of progress, we are obligated to reinvestigate all cures which offer relief whether religious or otherwise. We have today moved from universalism toward individualism.

B. The Return to a Christian Notion of Salvation

What did "salvation" originally mean as an offer to restore mental health? In forming a reply to this question, we should note that all Christians have not and do not agree on one precise meaning for "salvation." Yet in opposition to Becker's proposal, some features stand out: (1) A relation to God is required for effective salvation versus simply the use of human assistance; (2) This involves a transcendence of nature. That is, we admit that the means for our salvation are not totally available to us at will, which is the notion modern humanists fought against; (3) God has acted through revelation to open salvation to all who will accept it, but this depends on certain persons, scriptures, and the institutions that stem from these; (4) At least some who receive salvation find themselves radically transformed, returned to mental health. But this takes place by a power which comes from outside, not from inside nature. The action that restores is essentially done to them, although human instruments or intermediaries may be involved; (5) However, all this being said, we must admit that an interest in religion and a tendency to mental imbalance lie close together. It is not so simple a matter as to say that everyone is restored who has contact with religion. Since the pursuit of religion destroys some who become involved, this pursuit is a mixed factor in human life. Were this not so, we would not experience the intense feelings which arise when friends or family undergo a traumatic conversion to new religious movements. Many fear the cure all the while it is pursued.

But when it comes what are the therapeutic effects of salvation? How does it produce mental health, and do these results differ significantly from those obtained by secular procedures? The main factor in the religious situation, I believe, is that the person has come to feel burdened with guilt, however acquired, and this places his psychic life under a shadow. Those who still believe the promise of the Enlightenment will fight against the religious feeling of guilt as being "abnormal." However, Christianity contends that release from this oppression can come but only as a result of forgiveness. Essentially, this generous gift is thought to be divine in origin, although it may be administered by the human agents of religion. The return to mental health, then, involves our ability to lift the burden of guilt. Such a result is often reported as a return to wholeness. The one who suffers from guilt feels split and incapacitated because of the accumulated burden. The cleansing action of forgiveness releases psychic energy to function effectively rather than to imbed one deeper into self-recrimination. The man or woman acts and feels as if he or she has been made new.

It is this feeling of restoration to a lost original state that is most characteristic of salvation as an avenue to mental health. Popularly we call it to be "born again." Although not always rightly understood, this phrase is an accurate symbol for the person's restored state. Wrong actions and unsuccessful projects have burdened the individual to make him or her feel old too soon. Thus, salvation means a recovery of newness and the return to a sense of the innocence of youth.

Kierkegaard thought that innocence was not a virtue one should wish to recover, but much of Christian doctrine differs with him on this matter, in spite of the difference between "innocence" and "naivete". Mental illness is the state of carrying a burden too heavy to bear. Salvation is the release from that incapacitating burden. Adam's actions banished him from the Garden of Eden. He was doomed to suffer until such time as he could recover his lost state of innocence. That is why salvation is referred to as the state of "becoming a child again." The lost Garden of Eden is restored in the sense that one feels innocence recovered and no hinderance to the exercise of natural powers. Secular therapy explores our childhood states, but its aim is to carry the patient beyond them. Salvation claims that it is only by the return to an earlier innocent state, which all once shared, that mental health can be restored.

Of course, anyone who advocates following the religious life as a means to mental health has to admit that many who seek it never find it. Just as salvation lies near to destruction in the religious configuration, many who seek it become lost. Thus, a certain lack of control accompanies the religious way. The claim of psychiatry is to greater accuracy with its method.

To follow Christianity one needs to assent to much more than in following modern psychiatry. There is a pre-condition to sharing in its promised health. One need not "believe in" Freud or Jung to be cured by their methods, or so it seems. Thus, Christianity is not a "full rationalism," because it assumes that reason is as much a part of the problem as it is of the answer. Cure is often blocked by our belief in Becker's assertion (or Freud's) that reason alone should now take control of our lives. Confidence stems from our belief in the power to recreate ourselves in spite of the fact that society often corrupts us. Rational investigation, traditional Christianity believes by way of contrast, can never be more than a stage in the initial quest. Christianity asserts that reason, as such, does not move the emotions in the ways they need to be altered.

One difficulty which Christianity faces, in addition to its conflict between individual and universal, is that "salvation" is never full and complete. The "restored person" is only partially or provisionally returned to new life. The person may enjoy his or her release as if it were complete. But the notion of Jesus' "Second Coming" is a symbol for the fact that the present era must be brought to a close and the whole earth transformed before individual restoration can be complete and final. Thus, the individual who experiences salvation and the gift of a new life does so only by participating, in advance, in a world yet to be brought into existence. This partial or provisional nature of all Christian experience often leads to disappointment or loss. A first experience of joy moves easily to disappointment, particularly if the individual is unable to sustain his hope for the future and cannot continue his religious life in anticipation of a final transformation. Furthermore, in Christianity this new hope must be shared and passed on to others by specific acts to relieve their suffering. It cannot be held alone. It fades fast if not transferred.

This fragile and incomplete nature of salvation leads to the common phenomenon of disillusionment or even bitterness that often develops in the religious novice too soon after religious conversion and its experience of release. The new member of the religious group often expects something more complete and permanent than an indefinite transitional stage can offer. The joy of experiencing the return of mental health causes the receiver to count on more than has been promised. The human intermediary in this religious process may have made stronger or more absolute promises than the doctrine and past experience can support. Or, disciples may, in their enthusiasm, project greater powers of transformation onto the leader than anyone but God can provide. This explains the psychological necessity to claim a divine status for the "messenger of God". In addition, since God is at the center of all this and not something humanly knowable, the notorious elusiveness of divinity makes the search for mental health through salvation more a life-long pilgrimage than a permanent and present discovery. The issue is one of finding health and release in a situation of permanent quest.

Disillusionment sets in early in love affairs and in religious transformation.

As Ernest Becker illustrates, the age of Modern Science and rationalism hoped to open a route to mental health that was universally available, one under human control, one less involved in transcendence and more permanent in its effect. In addition to our previous discussion as to whether this project has succeeded, as we look over a record of psychiatry we must ask whether the human psyche is of such a nature that its mental health will always be volatile and vulnerable. One illustration will suffice to indicate the nature of this difficulty. As stated above, God's involvement in the process of salvation introduces added complexity as well as offering help. Many representatives of religion offer their road to salvation as secure, final, and seemingly easy. But when the human psyche faces God, the neatness of the offered solutions often fade away as one discovers how illusive and difficult God can be to deal with because of divinity's transcendence of human ways and norms. This is why "faith" is required to continue in any religious group. That is, release may come, but salvation is a matter which knows no final solution now.

Beyond all this lies the question of whether some, if not all, human consciousness demands, or is oriented to, a transcendence of the natural order. The modern age intended either to domesticate God, as Descartes did, or to place God outside nature, as Hume and Kant both did. This left them free to deal with the soul as a natural phenomenon. If for many human beings God is an unavoidable object of search, the human psyche remains open to transcendence in a way that predisposes it to heroic quests. Becker himself suggests this, but he hopes to keep it all within natural bounds. The tendency to look beyond the natural order prevents us from adjusting to a restricted and controllable sphere of activity. That which offers us new life and mental health is the same force which drives us continually beyond both ourselves and nature in a search for the divine. If this is our human situation, mental health is not easy to find or to maintain, and it can never be possessed with finality. Nevertheless, human life as an open-ended challenge can be exciting, once we overcome our natural disappointment in the failure of the Social Sciences to provide us with mental health on a universal and permanent basis, one within our control as modern scientists. Today the possibility of religious salvation can be pursued by every person, even though it is not necessarily an achieved state.

CHAPTER VI

THE REBIRTH OF MEANING:

THE HUMAN PROBLEM[14]

A. The New Social Sciences vs. an Age-Old Philosophy

With the rise of the Social Sciences came a tendency to think that philosophy would never again be involved in the healing of human beings or have much concern with the practical problems of people. Before the split into the division of academic fields which exists today, philosophy had been thought of as a source of help. Epicurus said: "Vain are the words of the philosopher which heals no suffering of man."[15] We know the followers of Plotinus lived together in a community and thought that following his guidance would provide an avenue of escape from life's problems. Philosophy was identified with the life of the church in the Middle Ages; the

---

[14]This chapter appeared in an earlier version in Zygon, Vol. 18, No. 1 (March 1983), pp. 83-95.

[15]In Fragments, 59.

church made its practical application an assured fact. With the coming of the Modern Age and the rise of science, all this changed. The Social Sciences were expected to deal with the human situation in a new and improved way that assured us greater success in improving the human condition. Freudianism is part of this trend. Pragmatism and existentialism are more recent movements attempting to restore philosophy's practical application.

If we want to appraise the success of the Social Sciences in their effort to take the guidance of humanity away from philosophy, Ernest Becker, in his The Birth and Death of Meaning[16] gives us a good account of the attempt to cure all human ills. However, Becker alters the early hope for a "pure science" by reintroducing philosophy into the picture. He admitted that philosophy could not be dispensed with, as was once attempted, but is still needed to provide our understanding of humanity. In another sense Becker is still an unreconstructed modernist. That is, convinced the Social Sciences have produced the basis on which all reform and renewal must rest: "We are today in possession of an excellent general theory of human nature... " (p. viii) as a result of the work of anthropology, sociology, psychology, and psychiatry.

The clue to Becker's optimism is that he thinks we no longer are trapped in the age-old situation of humanity as being defective because we are the only species in the universe that has "pushed self-exposure to such an

---

[16]The Free Press, New York, 1971. Second Edition.

advanced point that we are no longer a secret to ourselves" (Ibid.). Echoing the revolutionary cry of the Social Sciences, Becker believes that we are now in a position to free ourselves. "We are in possession of a mature scientific psychology that . . . is the most powerful critical weapon that we have for the potential freeing of men" (p. ix).

Although Becker's statement is filled with modern optimism, the interesting fact is that he rejects a rosy view of human nature. He stresses our darker side and recognizes both human evil and viciousness. In this sense, his assessment of the human condition is not far from traditional religious views of original sin. In this respect he differs from the Enlightenment thinkers who viewed the doctrine of sin as a major obstacle to reform and who believed theology had to be rejected. Becker is still optimistic about our ability to raise ourselves up with the aid of this new science. God is no longer to be held responsible for our condition; society is substituted as the responsible villain. If we can change society we can change ourselves. Jean Jacques Rousseau was wrong only in that he thought the task of reform was easy.

We can now complete the Enlightenment attempt to reform, and Becker's mission is to urge us to do so as quickly as possible. Erich Fromm and Otto Rank are Becker's heroes in this. True, our subject is humanity which is full of more frustrating complexity than the Enlightenment dreamed possible. Like God, who grew more puzzling as the medieval philosophical-theologians approached him, humankind has proved more baffling to us the longer we searched than the early moderns thought. The difference is that the study of God's ways of thought is a "learned ignorance," as Lucanus said. Studying divinity brings us not to a solution but to the depths of an abyss. Modern psychology, on the other hand, has aimed to complete the task once thought impossible.

"Man becomes man in a total celebration of himself," said Becker long before the age of narcissism was criticized. Yet Becker plots a "story of humanity" tracing our development from ape to humanist. This finally reaches an apex in symbolic behavior" (p. 6). With language and thought we have learned how to act in an extremely unpredictable environment; this is our "coming of age" (p. 12). The philogenic account of human development which Becker gives seems to him true and a key to achieving the understanding and control that gives us the power to release ourselves. For him speech symbolizes everything we call human (p. 80). Our major distinction as animals is that we are the only ones who are self-reflective. In opposition to the behaviorists, Becker stresses the reality of the inner world, and he thinks we now understand it well enough to control our inner life. The behaviorists thought we could only modify behavior if every action were external and thus observable.

Yet, Becker is convinced that we must pay for our favorable position in nature by constant anxiety. Our ability to withstand anxiety Becker labels as "heroic." His concept of ideal behavior is to be free from anxiety. To do this we have to pay a heavy price--restrict our experience (p. 55). Thus, we cannot be humanized without developing neurosis. This vulnerability should not be denied; it should be stressed because the feeling of guilt is natural to the human condition. This view allies Becker more with the Middle Ages than to the Modern Age.

We exchange a natural or animal sense of basic worth for a contrived or symbolic one. This is unavoidable if we wish to be human, but it also makes us vulnerable to self-condemnation. Without self-esteem we cannot act; we break down (p. 75). Creating self-esteem is Becker's avenue to achieving human salvation. Each-human-a-hero is Becker's solution. However, unlike Freud, he does not think that society forces neurosis upon us; rather, society is the very vehicle for heroism (p. 78). Here lies the root of Becker's optimism: Culture does not inhibit us; it releases us. If fully developed, cultural life is our salvation. True, some cultural systems hold us in bondage, but now that we understand our human goal there is no reason why they should continue to do so. If we are to act heroically we need self esteem, and society is the source. As Jean Paul Sartre said, now we alone create meaning in existence; we must find it for ourselves.

Culture's job is to construct a "meaningful hero system" for its members. That is the key to our newly opened pathway to escape our age-old bondage (p. 118). Yet, achieving Becker's goal depends on doing away with a sense of an invisible world. We must agree that all real experience exists on the level of the visible world alone (p. 120). If it does not, Becker believes we may continue to fear an unknown and become restless heroes. In order to gain control of all human nature for ourselves, we must postulate that what is visible is all that is real and that it can be controlled by us. He thinks modern westerners already have lost all belief in spiritual causality. If so this would enable us to ignore transcendence and apply all our effort to manipulate the visible world (Ibid.). Is this true? Do we have the agreement on this issue so that we can base our salvation from anxiety on it? Of course, we do have to eliminate fiction from our hero systems, and not place our trust in events which cannot become true. Becker realizes that many past beliefs have borne little relation to observable fact. For some reason, however, he thinks this past is behind us forever.

Human freedom is a fabricated entity. It is delicate and fragile for just that reason. We need to be disillusioned. Disillusionment removes the veil between us and reality and allows us to see our fate full face. Becker thinks our uniqueness, which also is the basis of his optimism rests on the fact that at last we stand face to face with reality. All who have gone before us have seen only a veiled reality; we see it as it is. Human meaning is not a given fact. It involves self-deception. We must accept that despair and the death of meaning are carried by humanity as a basic condition of being human (p. 140-41). This death of meaning is what Becker finds to be the core of the human problem; this is what must be overcome in order to achieve our self-salvation. We can face and overcome it by being a cosmic hero" (Ibid.). Friedrich Nietzsche thought that the heroes in society were few. This role is only for the super-humanly strong. However, Becker postulates a world built on the possibility of "every-human-a-hero." We can all achieve this by contributing to world life, in spite of death.

A person's character is a defense against impotence and the threat of madness (p. 144). Soren Kierkegaard believed this and turned to God. Becker postulates the same human dilemma, but he calls on us to turn to ourselves and to the culture we create. The question is: Can we self-create? What is the source for Becker's trust that we can do so? "This is the whole promise of Modern Science, that it would finally banish illusion" (p. 157). The two great sciences of sociology and psychology arose in the nineteenth century to fulfill the Enlightenment promise to establish interrelationships in the physical but also in the social and personal world. Why, then, is the burden of illusion still so much upon us? Becker thinks the answer is a twentieth century discovery. We had to find out scientifically "what caused people not to be able to see the true interrelationship of things" (Ibid.). And Becker believes this is precisely what modern psychology has discovered.

"The thing that prevents whole societies from seeing reality is the fictional nature of their hero systems" (p. 138). The aim of the Social Sciences is to come to grips with the fictions that constrain human freedom.

Becker has found the source of our release: "The findings of a mature psychology support the ideal of democratic man and reveal to him the causes of his failure" (p. 163). This knowledge shall make us a free, open and adaptable people. In theological terms, this is a modern Gnosticism based on a confidence in the Social Sciences. The new Garden of Eden offered to us depends for its fulfillment on eliminating all flaws in human nature. Becker is romantically optimistic on this point: "There is no inherent evil in man that would subvert the ideal of democracy" (p. 174). Of course, his scheme will not work unless we can rid ourselves of those faults which have fatally infected every good plan we have devised. However, Becker feels that the empirical data of psychology tells us that it is logical to pursue the ideal of democracy, now that humankind has come of age scientifically.

If we follow Becker, we will see religion and science as both agreeing that what is needed is a change in the basic structure of human nature. Science he claims now holds the key we need to accomplish this. Culture imposes restraints on humanity. The vast numbers who once followed religion were not sufficient to change human nature as a whole. Becker agrees with Karl Marx on this point. Large masses of people will have to turn from narrowness and delusion if whole societies are to be transformed. Evil Becker believes, stems not from humanity's wickedness but "from the way he was conditioned to see the world and to seek satisfaction in it" (p. 184). If this is true, we should now be able to control ourselves. The meager success religion has had shows us that the issue is whether we can change whole societies by design. If we are to do this, each individual must put self-esteem under his own control. "The person has to learn to derive his self-esteem more from within himself and less from the opinions of others" (p. 192). As Eve said of the snake as she protested her innocence to God, our flaws still come upon us from outside and not from within.

Unfortunately, being self-conscious causes despair. Becker says this stems partly from our unmitigated fear of death. Religion tells us this must be overcome. The difference is that Becker thinks we can overcome our despair alone. To accomplish this he proposes to create a human religion, one under our own control that offers the ideal "of what man might become by assuming the burden of his life" (p. 198). In a scientific age, human beings must move ahead under their own strength. If we have not been able to do this before on a scale sufficient to alter the human condition itself, how can we hope to do so now? Becker's faith rests on his belief that we have achieved self-understanding and have found a way to control or eliminate evil. At this point he sounds amazingly like Marx, who also claims the support of science, except that Becker is the child of the Enlightenment and counts on education and on new cultural attitudes to accomplish the necessary mass change. Both Marx and Becker count on the universal acceptance of one theory; they are certain of science.

What is fascinating about Becker's confidence in humankind's future is that he freely admits that, we have as yet failed to establish "a new science of humanity." "We have made no substantial advance in solving the basic dilemmas of social science since its founding in the last century," he writes in a later book (p. ix).[17] He believes that even the idea of forming a science of humanity is utopian by nature. Any form of utopianism out of the Enlightenment is just not possible. "We cannot bring into being a world in which sanity can unchallengeably reign and in which self-expansive human pleasure can be assured for the masses of men" (p. x)--this was Becker's hope in his earlier statements. He does not trust violent revolutions, as Marx does, because force simply leads to a centralized statism that crushes the human spirit. Yet still we must believe in the utopian ideal. Even if it does not achieve the hoped for great community of the human species, it may stop chaos.

"The best we can hope for is to avoid the death and decay of mankind," he concludes in a more subdued tone (p. xi). The modest task of this "utopian holding action" is to sustain humanity in the face of overwhelming and unmanageable forces, an altered goal that brings Becker into line with both Judeo-Christian and Eastern philosophies. In a stroke he has radically altered, if not abandoned, the revolutionary task of the Social Sciences. Sociology, as well as the Protestant "Social Gospel", was born out of the anguish of asking how to remedy the evils of the industrial society.

---

[17]The Lost Science of Man, George Brazillier, New York, 1971.

Today science is quiet and objective; Sociology began with a sense of human urgency. The tragedy is that, in order to become a legitimate science, Sociology had to renounce its revolutionary ambition to alter the state of humanity.

"The story of the discipline of sociology in America is the story of the triumph of science over a vision" (p. 29). The vision was to bring about the union of science and ethics, and it has haunted us for the last two hundred and fifty years, science revolted against the jurisdiction of the church over humanity, but what authority did they substitute? Rationalism as a philosophy proposed to overcome the pain and unhappiness of life. Its followers needed a secular morality that all persons of good will could agree upon. Is there such a thing? Evil had to be taken away from theology and placed in the hands of science. Marx's economic view of humanity is too narrow. Instead Becker believes he can take in all of art, culture, and religion and still find the needed unified vision. The question is: "How could the sciences themselves supply a unitary vision to replace the lost medieval one?" (p. 35).

Becker does not scorn the unity of the Middle Ages; he views such unity as a necessity to form any ideal society. However his new society must be guided by a unified scientific view of humanity. Is it the social system itself, not human nature, that causes evil? If so, that can be altered and controlled. The life-meanings that move us are symbolically contrived. If we come to recognize this, we can learn the formula and thus create the meaning needed for life, since according to Becker's account it never was given from heaven. Yet he admits that the rise of anthropology has stressed the diversity of the human species, not its unity. If one theory simply arises from the data before us, the problem becomes one of explaining our differences, which anthropology set out to catalogue in all their variety. Once we realized this, a moral crisis was at hand. Becker laments: "The medieval world view had loosened its hold on society, and now there was nothing to replace it" (p. 116).

Our goal is to provide a new system of morality, but Becker admits this cannot be done unless "you have a unification of the various sciences into a single scheme" (Ibid.). Otherwise, in science as in life, all is disjointed. True, but except for wishing, what is the evidence that such a unity will emerge? Becker admits that a great deal depends on how much we want to use Social Science to instigate deep social change. If you want to do this, you first have to believe in the ideal of a unified and agreed scientific law (p. 136). Ironically, this does not sound much different from the medieval church's demand for belief as a prior condition for salvation.

History will not support our social ideals, Becker concedes, and general empirical law is subject to many exceptions as well. We first must "accept a certain moral and critical stance toward present conditions" (p. 137). What guarantees that this "moral and critical stance" will be one for all of us? Can this outlook become uniform and instigate massive change any more than the religions of the world have been able to unite us? Becker opts for Rousseau's moral-organizing principle (p. 139). But what leads him to believe any significant number of persons will make the same leap of faith? We need, Becker repeats, a secular moral code that answers the problem of the origin of evil in society. Yet what has he told us about the history of the social sciences (except that they have failed to accomplish this to date) that would lead us to expect the emerging of such a universally acceptable account? The result would seem to be various forms of individualism. And unlike Marx, Becker is suspicious of all forms of state control, and so he cannot opt for that avenue to create uniformity in society.

Becker's most crucial assumption is that "man is born pliable and natural and is shaped by his society" (p. 151). If this is true, it offers one basis for hope. What leads him to think humans are that pliable, except that many have been taught to accept this as a basic premise. Perhaps we are more fixed in our nature such that major transformations cannot be self-induced.

If we need a new myth for the meaning of life, what makes us thinks it lies within our power to create it? Becker admits his vision is a dream, but all he says is he cannot do without it. Or more precisely, he says he does not seem to know any other way to achieve a restored humankind except to hang on to the Enlightenment vision, even after he has documented its continual failure. It is as if he reached the end of his analysis and found that no evolution has really taken place. He has become so used to the idea that progress is possible that he cannot abandon what seems like his last best hope. He is correct to say that the human problem is the rebirth of meaning, but where are we to go after Becker's devastating critique of the Enlightenment and our realization of what has or has not come from it?

B.   Can Theology Provide a Renewed Source of Meaning?

If the vision of what the Social Sciences might do has failed to materialize, and if we cannot join Marx in his optimism about the power of revolution and a new state to produce fundamental change, what options are open to us? Psychiatry as a science hoped to produce massive social change by working individually. Freud thought he could accomplish this goal on the basis of an accepted theory. But Becker does not think that this optimism has proved justified. One option always open for us is to return to religion, and there is some evidence this is occurring; it is the quiet cynicism, the despair into which many have slipped. Also, the second option is to return to individualism and find meanings in small groups. A reservation is that promoting individual change actually thwarts the goal of massive social alteration. A third option is offered by the descendants of G. W. F. Hegel who see art and aesthetics as a road to salvation. If we put too great a burden on aesthetic experience to create meaning for our lives, we may strain art beyond the limits of its powers.

By way of an alternative, let us re-explore the theological dimension. The Enlightenment and those who objected to religion's dominance as a provider of human meaning, did so primarily on two grounds: (1) That religion was stultifying to human freedom and thwarted the development of humanity's potential; and (2) that science has placed in our hands tools which allow a mass change in the human condition more so than any religion accomplished. We are essentially face-to-face with a modern Prometheus. Science gives us new and powerful tools which allow us to break the lock and wrest power from the Gods permanently. We wanted to control our own destiny, not just for a time and for a few, but for the future and for us all. We know that this was formerly not possible. The belief that we entered a new age inspires confidence for the future.

If the Christian God is omnipotent and omniscient, the eclipse of human freedom is required. In our struggle to be free in the Modern World, it often appeared that God must be eliminated if we were to gain our liberty. Sartre believed this. Not all have concurred but many have, particularly those who were influenced by scientific possibility. The conflict between science and religion has often centered on the question of setting us free to govern our own future. The revolutionaries who based their hope on the Social Sciences recognized that in the past a stable God provided the meaning for human significance, but they were confident that their new powers could provide substitutes. Meaning as well as freedom had to pass over into our control. Once free of God's domination, the human spirit could create its own meaning, we thought.

If God was banished as a source of meaning in life because divinity was too deterministic, could the Gods return if they were pluralistic rather than monolithic and if they embodied human indeterminacy rather than being opposed to it? Looking over the history of theology, the notion that there is a single view of God's nature appeared late on the scene. It is an over-simplification and seems more the work of human desire than divine dictate. Thus, if we redraw the model of the divine to reflect the variety actually found in religious history, and if we introduce contingencies into the divine life itself, there is no reason to deny God's existence in order to be free. In fact, it is quite possible that such a view of divinity will stimulate self-reliance rather than hinder it, since our freedom would be modeled on God's own. We cannot accept a single, inherited notion of God without criticism. The flexibility located within God's nature encourages us to establish our own form of stability.

In regard to the objection to religion that the Social Sciences have unleashed new power, we need to look at where the sciences stand today and how scientists conceive of their task. There is little evidence that contemporary physical scientists think of themselves as about to reach a final theory and gain acceptance for it. Whatever science has accomplished, it has not united behind one theory and seems not likely to do so. Science has produced technology and new discoveries but not a unified theory of humanity. Furthermore, human values seem to be less held in common but are more diverse. The more sophisticated the science, the more it discards the plan to reconstruct social consciousness as demanded by reformers such as Marx and Freud.

Two factors should concern us if theology is to return as a source of human meaning. First, our picture of the divine must not restrict human potential or arbitrarily limit human freedom. The divinity we encounter must be a God who is at home with contingency and willing to restrict divinity's powers, at least temporarily, to allow human beings to work out their own future. Neither omnipotence nor omniscience need be abandoned, as some have proposed, but they must be reinterpreted. God may still be perfect, but the notion of "perfection" cannot be identified with the idea of completion and actuality, as it was by Aristotle and Thomas Aquinas. Divinity can be redrawn in new images rather than abandoned. Some notions of human freedom which call for the denial of God, such as Sartre's probably are too extreme and are themselves in need of revision. We have not vindicated the confidence we thought we could place in ourselves had we gained unrestricted freedom.

The other factor which must be considered if theology is to become a renewed source of human meaning is our view of science. Looking back, it is clear that there never was one view of science. Some of the Modern Age had hoped for one view so that philosophy and theology could become complete. The issue at stake is whether science, however conceived, is sufficient as a producer and guardian of human meaning. Marx argued that science is the primary source of human meaning in the Modern World, but a glance at the development of science shows it has retreated from that role rather than asserted it.

Can a new vision of the divine as the source of human freedom, plus a reevaluation of the view of science that eliminated God as the provider of meaning in the name of human progress, allow the Gods to return from exile? Of course, the Gods have only been absent in certain philosophical and scientific circles whence they were banished in the name of creating a new society. Divinities have been in hiding or living with the common people, and they reemerge about as often as they are banished by decree. However, the absence of divinity in intellectual circles is not unimportant. When the Gods are in disrepute with the intelligentsia, we live a split life. We may feel their power, and yet we are half afraid to admit it for fear of being laughed at.

It is therefore important that the return of the Gods be intellectually grounded and accompanied by new theologies which do not simply repeat old tales. When the nature of divinity was thought to be fixed and static, a "perennial theology" was appropriate. If the Modern World set the Gods free at the same time that it freed us from religion, then a rapid change in theological conceptions would not be considered strange but would be expected. This might make the life of religion less comfortable than if theology remained fixed as an unchanging doctrine. To stress freedom in the life of religion offers just as much challenge to the Modern World as banning it would. If for a time we sought to enhance human meaning by freeing us from religion and its Gods, it would be a twist of fate if science failed to produce the sought for meaning. Our rebirth of meaning should prove quite compatible then with the return of theology. New conceptions of divinity breed new challenges to human minds. Evidently meaning can be reborn in human life in more ways than were thought possible in the early years of science.

C.   Metaphysics as the Provider of Meaning in Human Life

Becker's astute analysis of the rise of the Social Sciences (and their goal to replace philosophy and cure humankind) makes it clear that the project was not free of assumptions. It was based on its own metaphysical first principles which have unfortunately not proved exclusively true. Becker thinks the human revolution can still be accomplished by adopting a uniform science of humanity. However if this is not taking place, we must suspect that all human meaning is "metaphysically dependent." That is, significance is only given to human life if one vision of the world or another is accepted for a time and draws its energy from those who adopt it, not because it is exclusively true. The only problem is that the reformers in the Social Sciences thought the source of meaning could be given a final form, thus providing a stability metaphysics cannot offer.

However, if such unity of theory is not achievable and thus plurality in theory remains, the discipline of metaphysics returns as "our basic science." That discipline outlines and compares our first principles, and does without an assumption that one view of reality will come to embrace all others. Of course Hegel believed in a metaphysics of process," that a particular metaphysics reveals reality progressively and cumulatively. That is, he assumed that not all theories have acceptable alternatives. However, if we want a metaphysics to sustain meaning in social reality, we must first decide about the nature of metaphysics. In doing so we cannot yield to Hegel's view, or to any theory, without a prior comparative study. This means we must spread out all the classical and contemporary options before us. As long as a variety of alternatives in our theories remain, we know that human meaning and our vision of social reality can never be finally one. We also know that the rebirth of human meaning depends, not on the physical sciences or even the social sciences but on our willingness to keep metaphysics alive as a fundamental human enterprise.

Concerning our suggestion in the preceding section of this chapter about the restored role of theology, we also know that our conception of divinity (if we seek to provide meaning from that source) is "metaphysically dependent". There is not now, and really never has been, only one view of the divine nature. This means no contemporary suggestion concerning God can prove entirely adequate. In scripture God has been reported to say many things, some strange, some profound, but God never has given an endorsement of one metaphysics as adequate and final for the description of the divine life. Plurality may be necessary where divinity is concerned, which means no rest in our quest for meaning and for God.

If theology is also subject to theoretical instability and lack of finality, how can it support human meaning and establish social reality, much less give final authority to religion? Evidently, human meaning does not depend on achieving finality in theory. Social reality seems able to support human endeavors without demanding uniformity in theory. True, since we are humans with inescapable fears, we are prone to sin, a tendency Becker finds innate. Wars and political or religious attacks will go on. Perhaps this destructive conflict is induced by our frantic effort to use force to overcome our human instability. The social reformers hoped to end destructive human conflict. Perhaps the history of metaphysics tells us that reconstruction is a constant necessity, given the fragile nature of human means and social reality.

CHAPTER VII

THE GODS RETURN

A.   When Will the Gods Return?

Since the Gods departed without much ceremony, we should not expect
a public celebration of their return.   Furthermore, Gods have always been
arriving and departing.   Is there one among us who would deny that there
have been times and places where the presence of divinity has been felt
overwhelmingly?   Shrines have been erected to commemorate such spots.
This is enough to let us know that human nature and the nature of divinities
are such that the Gods are never uninterruptedly present to all men and
women.   We must, then attempt to learn "the rhythm of the divine" or else be
continually disappointed when the Gods prove absent when we expect or hope
for their presence.

Yet we have been speaking of a prolonged period of the absence of the
Gods.   How can this be so if what we have just said is true of their mode of
presence?   In the first place what we have been experiencing is a public
absence of the sense of divinity--an intellectual ban on such experiences in
many places, as well as a political banishment from countries in which it was

thought that divinity's presence would thwart the state. In addition, the Gods have neither manifested themselves according to a fixed schedule nor appeared equally to all peoples at all times. We experience dry seasons religiously as well as ecstatic periods of revival. If this were not so, we would not use the terms "revival" and "renewal" where religion is concerned, nor would we need "faith" if divine presence were a consistent matter.

Nevertheless, in spite of the ban in some intellectual circles, and the official political prohibition against the Gods in certain countries, we know that the experience of divine presence has never ceased in the hearts of some people. Of course, the numbers have recently been lower than at other times when officials sanctioned a transcendental presence. Like Thomas in the New Testament account, we insecure human beings demand public recognition to bolster our doubt. We have long known that a God's presence is mediated by, if not dependent on, public symbols. If the public symbols of religion decrease or are banned, our internal sense often is insufficient to sustain a divine presence. We often feel an external stir but we need support if we are to sustain this against a neutral or an alien environment.

It is clear we have been living through a period of the absence of the Gods from the public scene they once occupied. To report this is not to say whether this is all good or all bad. The presence of divinities has led to destruction and violence as well as to healing and peace. The negative side of religious repression was well known to those who proposed a prohibition on religion in the name of human progress. Yet after two or three centuries of trying, with only partially favorable results, we are forced to ask whether any ban against the Gods has been or can be successful. Since the problems in human life have by no means disappeared or human nature transformed to a new and higher plane by science, it must be that religion was not responsible for all our ills.

If the Gods have never departed completely from human experience, and if they still frequently reappear on an individual level should we not lift the public ban which the Modern Age imposed and allow the Gods an intellectual and a public standing once again? Of course we need not be indiscriminate in our public celebration of the Gods' return. In any general rejoicing, as the censorship is lifted after so long a ban on religion one should be sensitive to the devastating potential religion has always displayed if uncontrolled. All aspects of all Gods are not pleasant or conducive to human development. So as the Gods approach our primary problem is to learn to select among the available (i.e., those who appear to us) for qualities which heal and restore rather than destroy. The Hebrews knew well enough the ferocious aspects of an angry God, and we should not overlook this potential in any divinity we approach.

To our question "when will the Gods return?" we must answer: (1) They have never ceased to return; they are among us unrecognized. (2) If the Gods' public presence is to be recognized as legitimate once more, we must do our best to see that this has the most positive and the fewest negative results. We learn from our religious history where God and religion seem to lead to destructive consequences. An enlightened age seeks to avoid a repetition. (3) Theology must again become "the queen of the Sciences." We realize that some theologians wanted to claim control of all science. The wisdom behind the pre-eminence of theology was a necessity for a constant and careful intellectual scrutiny of the divine nature. It takes training to distinguish the good and bad in divinities, and such eternal vigilance is the price of peace in our religious life. Theologians not only speak about Gods; they must judge among them.

We must recognize the mistaken premise in modern humanity's denial: We were sure that the Gods could be banished in the name of science; they would depart quietly to the comfort of all. There has been scattered economic, human improvement but not on a universal scale as was hoped would result if religion vanished. The quality of our life has refused scientific control and even deteriorated to violence. The absence of public religion cannot be said to have improved our lives. Religious belief alone has sometimes made life tolerable, in the face of humanity's unrelenting cruelty. Our human record is as mixed as ever. In this case there is no need to keep the Gods in exile in the name of human improvement, in spite of the harm some religions have reeked in the past.

Can we attain the spiritual sensitivity we sometimes have had which we so much need and which is to hard to develop? It is necessary to do so if we are to prepare for the Gods' return with discrimination. The great religious seers knew how difficult it was to locate a God among the Gods who answered their religious needs, or even more important how difficult it is to know exactly what our spiritual needs are. The early Moderns thought the idea of God to be one and to have an agreed history. Thus, if any difficulty with religion appeared, the answer was to ban God. As a result of such simple thinking we became insensitive to the plural nature of divinities and the demand placed on us to discriminate and to locate the right God for the right religious need, difficult as this may be and still subject to failure. The penalty for our failure in the theological task is not the absence of all divine presence but a loss of our sense of discrimination. This can become destructive for the human spirit.

If we have not made much human progress and if humankind does not seem likely to reform itself, there is less reason to exclude the Gods. We might as well enjoy their presence openly and tremble at their wrath again. But the Gods departed. In this respect their ability to return intellectually to some status in academic circles is a crucial question. Can we restore theology to its link with philosophy so that it is no longer necessary to be an atheist by being a philosopher? Philosophy must be reconstructed and its secular modern image altered. There is no longer any need for philosophers to be skeptics in the name of leading the revolution in human nature and founding ideal societies.

If human beings have remained the same in spite of external revolutions, philosophy need not be wedded to one program in the name of progress. As the Gods return to us, so do all the ancient and classical forms of philosophy. This is not to say that philosophy is doomed to revert to the past. New forms are possible. It is just that no anticipated human progress forces philosophy to take one form against another. We have lived with the wide-spread prejudice that either we accepted philosophy in a modern form or rejected modernism. In some sense that was true. But with the return of the Gods, the dream of inevitable and non-retractable progress is gone. We are free to be ourselves as philosophers, as well as to think religiously without apology.

Just how and when the Gods return in fact depends on our receptivity and our developed sensitivity to divine presence; no intellectual goals necessarily exclude them. Since divinity's public presence depends on adequate symbolic representation, the day of the Gods return will depend on human inventiveness in preparing the vehicles by which their presence can be known and recognized. Our ability to symbolize and to give body to the divine has grown rusty with disuse, at least on a spiritual level. Thus, we must devise new exercises and train ourselves in religious disciplines before the way of return is clear. Their absence has, then, been a failure in preparation on our part because of the scientific and intellectual ban, as well as a failure of the Gods to be near at hand. The time of the return can be of our own choosing now that the fixed barriers have crumbled in the failure of the modern revolutionary program.

We must, however, tremble as well as rejoice, or else we show a lack of awe before the divine presence. Human awe in the face of divinity was once set aside because humankind for time stood in awe of its own nature and what it expected to accomplish in the Age of Reason and by means of science. Now that awe has partially turned to terror over our own destructive potential; awe regarding powers transcending our own is once again possible and natural. Our hope to remove all terror from human existence has not proved possible. In consequence we must be careful that the terror of the divine does not destroy us as the Gods' reenter. In addition, we sought to eliminate alienation in human experience. But once we find our own nature to be the source of alienation, find it beyond elimination, we must be careful that our alienation is not made more intense by the Gods' return.

How can one prevent a sense of constant alienation in the face of divine presence? Those moderns were right who thought that religion took our attention away from ourselves and placed it on deities we could never hope to imitate. "If there are Gods, how can we stand not to be one?" Some alienation is necessary and inevitable in the presence of the Gods. But the same is true in confronting ourselves, as we have learned with some sadness. We cannot as we hoped radically alter our own nature. Our choice apparently is not to eliminate alienation but to learn how to deal with it. Perhaps we can even do so creatively in the way Kierkegaard and the existentialists recommend. Why not be lifted out of ourselves by a divine ecstasy, then? If we can be, we learn how to confront the Gods and the sense of alienation which that encounter initially produces?

Our problem seems to center on how to handle what is our own rather than to transform it beyond its original nature. In such a situation, one God or another (but certainly not all) can be of help. After all, this claim has been at the core of the traditional assertion of religion. It is only if we hope to transform our original given human nature that the Gods become irrelevant. If we have no choice but to be ourselves, we might as well do it with as much dignity, and in concert with religious tradition, as possible. All else is modern arrogance. The presence of the Gods impedes our intellectual progress and reform movements only if we assume we can deny our original nature. If we could do this, we might hope to eliminate our early and pervasive fascination with the life of the Gods. If not, then becoming close to one God can be a stimulus to intellectual endeavor and not restrictive.

We have been told that we have come of age and thus are sufficient without divine support. We were also told that we live in a "secular city," one now devoid of all religion. Actually, we have always been sufficient as human beings. Any divine support we have received, or are likely to receive, has always contained a large element of human mediated dependence. The

Gods seldom appear immediately or support us directly. Churches and religious leaders may offer direct support, sometimes helpful, sometimes misleading, but the respectable divinities are more indirect in their techniques and more subtle. Religiously we have always been on our own. We have not just recently come of age, although some come to religious maturity and independence at different times. True, the church has not been as prominent in human affairs as it has in the past. But to be somewhat independent of religious institutions may not be a bad thing, and ecclesiastical independence says little about our relationship to the Gods.

Similarly, cities have been secular at their core, although some romantic American and religious leaders have sometimes thought otherwise. Church ecclesiastics have often had more prominent political roles than democracy allows. But until the world is transformed, cities will always be secular and the Gods hard to find on the streets no matter how obscure they may be visually. The return of the Gods will make little difference to the traffic pattern in our cities. It will be silent and inward not like the arrival in town of a President or a St. Patrick's Day parade.

When the Gods return, then, depends on us. And they will not arrive at once, since each one must be made real in our individual experience. Being plural and hidden by nature, the Gods do not conform to human wishes, neither religious or scientific. Little in their past behavior indicates that they appear on demand or in convenient forms. But since we know that divinity has never departed totally and is no longer blocked by intellectual and revolutionary programs that demand the Gods' absence as a condition for success, the barriers in our minds can also disappear. Then, as we have said, we must cultivate the soil left fallow for so long and increase our powers of receptivity, all the while not expecting any noisy celebration to herald their arrival.

It would of course be easier for us (and for church hierarchies) if the Gods drew lots and allowed only one divinity to return publicly. But having been ever plural in the heart of humans, the Gods are no more likely to reform their nature along singular lines than humankind is likely to cease its self-defeating ways. Does this mean that we cannot look to a God to save us? Certainly we can. We just must be sure to seek out a divinity with sufficient power to accomplish what is promised and not expect the road to be easy, obvious, or immediately achievable. The return of the Gods by no means signals the end of all our problems. It only means that our religious struggles can take place in the open again and need not be hidden. Life can become more difficult when Gods appear. The return of the Gods also means that there is no longer any intellectual stigma attached to seeking a way to speed the return of the Gods into our individual lives.

B.   How Shall We Receive Them?

With a touch of sadness. After all, their return signals the end of the Modern Era as well as an end to the dreams of the Modern World. It was not so bad, after all, to propose to eliminate evil from human nature, cure our mental and physical ills, and create ideal new societies that provide for all our needs. Could these great goals have been achieved, to banish the Gods would not have been too great a price to pay. To admit religion once again as a legitimate intellectual calling, and theology as the most noble enterprise, is also to abandon our goal to explain everything on the level of a science. We would do so if we could but we cannot, evidently.

Yet, we can receive the Gods' return with a bit of rejoicing too. Our spiritual life did not disappear in the Modern Era as some had predicted it would. It merely went underground, sometimes ran dry and remained unfulfilled. Thus, the return of the Gods offers satisfaction to long unfulfilled desires. It expands our horizons and stretches life beyond our present plane. And if there are new concepts of God which we can discover, we might find the Gods more satisfying to us than before. Our life may become less secure and less in our control with the advent of the Gods, but it may also be more exciting. If we could create ideal societies populated by newly molded men and women, it would be worth surrendering our old Gods. However, if we only succeed in spoiling each new society because we have not changed human nature we should enjoy the excitement offered by divine pursuits.

John Dewey's A Common Faith[18] offers a good example of the hopes we may have to abandon with the return of the Gods. As is well known, Dewey was not a religious man. Even though he believed the need for religion had been eliminated, he thought we needed some equivalent to replace function in society. Becker and Dewey both thought that "the advance of culture and science has completely discredited the supernatural and with it all religions that were allied with belief in it" (p. 1). Dewey did not want to argue for a return to religion; far from it. But he did think a human factor could be preserved which he called "religious," although it was to be entirely dependent upon our common experience. As an advocate of the new Social Sciences, he felt that we could "modify conditions so that they will be accommodated to our wants and purposes" (p. 16).

Dewey summed up his proposal to replace older religions in this way: "There is such a thing as faith in intelligence becoming religious in quality" (p. 26). "Any activity pursued in behalf of an ideal end against obstacles and in spite of threats of personal loss because of conviction of its general and enduring value is religious in quality" (p. 27). His trust, like Becker's, was in the new emerging sciences: "New methods of inquiry and reflection have become for the educated man today the final arbiter of all questions of fact, existence, and intellectual authority" (p. 31). Dewey is willing to have a God,

---

[18]Yale University Press, New Haven, 1934. All page references are to this edition.

but he redefines divinity: "It is this active relation between ideal and actual to which I would give the name "God"" (p. 51). Now, some fifty years later, we have to ask Dewey if this modern replacement for religion has in fact occurred. If not, Dewey and Becker are both linked to the world that aimed to exclude the Gods and to replace them with humanly constructed ideals.

John Dewey stands behind Ernest Becker, and Descartes stands behind them both as one of the fathers of the Modern Age. Dewey and Becker place their whole faith in a new methodology to be achieved by Modern Science, and it is this which gives them their confidence that we will be able to achieve our ideals where others could not.

Descartes' Discourse on Method[19] offers a model of this confidence. He believes reason to be equal in all persons and that all our differences come merely from conducting our thoughts in diverse ways (p. 1). Were this the case, adopting a common method could be expected to remove all human differences, and the Moderns were all hopeful that this new method could be confirmed. Mathematics, of course, became for them a model of certitude. One could almost believe that every question had a mathematical solution; one had equal confidence that a new methodology could eliminate our differences.

Of course, the great assumption always was that truth is singular not multiple. In similar fashion, there must be one agreed notion of God and not

---

[19]Trans. Veitch, Open Court Publishing Co., La Salle, Illinois, 1946. All quotations are from this edition.

many Gods. Otherwise, the hope to achieve our goals now will be frustrated. Descartes hoped that clarity and distinctness in any idea will provide its test of truth (p. 19). And this might work if we could agree on what constitutes "clarity" and "distinctness". Also, his proposal assumes that the world was so constructed that whatever is clear and distinct is true. But what if the maker of the universe was not a rationalist? Proposing to test all ideas for clarity and distinctness has not opened the world to much greater understanding and certainly it has not led to much improvement. The great assumption (perhaps arrogance) always is: "That there is nothing beyond our reach nor so hidden that we cannot discover it" (p. 20). Such optimism is today called into doubt by the course of human history since Descartes' time.

Descartes proposed in his now famous criterion of the "Light of Reason," that "God has endowed each of us with some Light of Reason by which to distinguish truth from error" (p. 29). In spite of what some manage to discern and to report to us, such universal optimism does not seem warranted by subsequent events. It seems more as if the Gods present an intriguing, insolvable puzzle, not that God has set out a single path to truth for us all. God, as we all know, was central to Descartes' plan to provide certainty. This is strange, given our long-standing arguments over God and the opposition of the entire mystical tradition to any final understanding of divinity. Descartes and Dewey of course believe in an underlying evolution in human affairs which gradually works to raise us above old difficulties.

But, evaluating Descartes, Dewey and now Becker, such optimism in human evolution seems unwarranted.

If so, how shall we receive the Gods as they return? Studying Dewey we learn that we have not succeeded in replacing the supra-natural or in substituting for it a set of human ideals that spring from common experience. We learn from Descartes that we must receive the Gods as plural and we must not hope for a final unifying concept. We surrender our hope that the only source of our differences lies in the failure to apply a method not previously available. We should receive the Gods as unsympathetic to our human ambition to impose a final rationalism, as not allowing all our differences to be dissolved in some common methodology. The problem lies not in our failure to postulate ideals or to develop methodologies but in the plural and transcendent nature of all divinity. So we must receive the Gods without illusion of final resolution.

Rationalist thought which influenced the Modern World was not entirely Christian. As a Jew, Spinoza is an example of the way the modern hope transcended national and religious boundaries. In On the Improvement of the Understanding,[20] Spinoza suggested that "nothing regarded in its own nature can be called perfect or imperfect" (p. 6). If so, all is reduced to one nature, and the Gods can neither be distinct from humans, nor perfect, nor

---

[20]Edited by James Gutman, Hafner Publishing Co., New York, 1949. All page references are to this edition.

transcendent. If our minds must work on two or more planes at once, finality in human understanding will be more difficult if not impossible. We remain caught between two worlds that do not come into one focus. On the other hand, Spinoza believes that we can simply inspect any idea and discover its truth (p. 120). We could then ignore the transcendental. Nothing finally is beyond us.

The confidence of the Modern Age appears again when Spinoza says that "all confusion arises from the fact that the mind has only partial knowledge of a thing" (p. 21). But this can be over come. For centuries we have been sure that information would accumulate and that doubt would eventually be put to rest. Doubt never comes from any object outside the mind, Spinoza is sure (p. 27). If true, this presents the possibility of removing doubt by refining the mind. There is nothing positive about false or fictitious ideas, Spinoza believes (p. 37). If there were anything positive in false ideas, the source of our difficulty would be partially beyond our control. Knowing, as we do, that Spinoza's hopes for the resolution of all doubt has not materialized, we should receive the Gods back, even while being aware that their presence hinders our final understanding. The source of some human obscurity comes from the Gods and in that sense is not completely within our control.

Of all the Moderns who have proposed to revolutionize human nature, none has had wider effect than Karl Marx. If Descartes' proposal to eliminate human uncertainty rested on a plan to domesticate God into a simple, rational idea, Marx's revolution depended on a final edict to banish the Gods. Thus, for no one and for no proposal could the return of the Gods be more crucial than for Marx and the Marxist program. If others find differing Gods returning from those they expected or hoped for, then Marx's whole plan must be radically revised. The "Manifesto of the Communist Party," which he wrote with Friedrich Engels,[21] is probably his most widely known single short work. Engels sums up Marx's fundamental proposition: "Every historical epoch and prevailing mode of economic production and exchange and the social organization necessarily following from it form the basis upon which is built up, and from which alone can be explained, the political and intellectual history of that epoch" (p. 4).

Marx believed that the whole history of humankind has been a history of class struggles and that social evolution has brought humanity to a crisis in his time. Obviously, the Gods have little to do with explaining either history or human nature and so should cease to be a concern. He believed we now have in our possession the only key we need for self-understanding; this was recently revealed. The founding of America becomes, not a pilgrimage of the religiously persecuted seeking freedom of worship, but a paving of the way to establish the world market (p. 8). Marx thought the capitalist-industrial need

---

[21]English edition of 1888 as reprinted by Fever, editor, in Marx and Engels Basic Writings on Politics and Philosophy. Doubleday/Anchor, New York, 1959. All page references are to this edition.

for a constantly expanding market had brought us to a unique time in human history, one that cut us off from all previous eras or modes of human understanding.

With the development of modern machinery and the division of labor "the world of the proletarians has lost all individual character and, consequently, all charm for the workman" (p. 14). Because of this "the proletariat alone is a really revolutionary class" (p. 17). This being true, it is only here where we can expect any change of alleviation in our situation. Since the bourgeoisie cannot help but aggravate the situation, "what the bourgeoisie produce, above all, is its own grave diggers" (p. 20). And the even more fundamental assumption which Marx held, but which Engels did not note, perhaps because he shared it and thus thought it obvious, is the premise of a dialectical necessity governing all history. If such a dialectic is absolute, the fall of the bourgeoisie "and the victory of the proletariat are equally inevitable" (Ibid.).

Marx also assumed that we would witness a progressive elimination of national boundaries and national or ethnic consciousness. "The working men have no country." "National differences and antagonism between peoples are daily more and more vanishing" (p. 26). Marx believed utopias are possible: "When . . . class distinctions have disappeared and all production has been concentrated in the hands of a vast association of the whole nation, the public power will lose its political character" (p. 29). "It will have swept away the conditions for the existence of class antagonisms and of classes generally, and will thereby have abolished its own supremacy as a class" (Ibid.). To accomplish this force is a necessity: "They openly declare that their ends can be attained only by the forcible overthrow of all existing social conditions" (p. 41). However, let us not argue with Marx/Engels as to whether what they said is correct or incorrect. Let us simply ask: If the Gods return, what does this mean for their program, and how should the Gods be received under Marxism?

The first thing to note is that Marx could be right in every assertion and still humankind's problems would not disappear under Marxist rule. Why and how? Because one unspoken premise of Marx is that all human ills can be traced to one source. Thus, if we alter that one condition, all human difficulties will disappear he thought. Let us assume for a moment that Marx was partially right in his analysis of the economic situation of his time. Some revolutions were effected and some economic improvements were made. Why then did the hoped for radical change in human nature and in the human situation not materialize? To change one condition is not sufficient to change human nature, since a multitude of factors shape us. Furthermore, given evil and human self-destruction, we are masters at creating new difficulties as fast as old ones are eliminated.

Like Descartes, Spinoza, and Dewey, Marx hoped to find a single strand in human nature that would be subject to universal and rational control.

Evidently human nature and the world (not to mention all the Gods) were not so simply designed. Like Descartes, Marx makes all things clear, but the clarity of the vision each induces in his reader is artificial. It is the product of a human hope for clarity and simplicity. Unfortunately it is neither an accurate reflection of the immense complexity of factors we face nor reverberatory of the tendency we have to transcend nature. "Economic production and exchange" is a factor in human nature but by no means the only one. For many it is perhaps not the most important. Life would be simpler if Marx's basic assumptions were wholly true, but little commends its truth. It is Marx's wish.

Undoubtedly class struggles exist, but can the explanation of all human history be reduced to that one phenomenon? If we succeed in ameliorating class struggle by revolution, and still fail to solve all human ills then this should tell us that the cause of human struggles are manifold and irreducible. Some causes are purely immanent in human nature and perhaps not universal. Marx's rationalism and his hope to pin-point a solution led him to assume a simple cause which neither reality nor history have manifested since the first communist revolution. Furthermore, both the inevitability of history and the dialectic governing this inevitability are even more difficult assumptions. Their absence means that predictability in human affairs cannot be the science many hoped it could be. Thus, if one class distinction disappears the outcome is still not an inevitable utopia but the development of new and perhaps even less desirable distinctions between human beings. Sometimes even terror not peace results when old powers are overturned. When one institutional change does not bring the desired utopia into existence, repression can become an instrument of a frustrated rationalism--trying to achieve by force that which did not come naturally.

Marx's single-mindedness, however, made him fail to see that force can corrupt human nature as well as destroy what blocks our progress. Thus, force is always a two-edged sword and not a magnificent surgeon's scalpel cutting out cancer, as Marx hoped it would be. If the men and women who wield the new power are no better as persons than those they replaced, then our gain may be in new varieties of corruption. Marx counted on eliminating the source of human evil and corruption and in creating new beings to carry out reforms. Unfortunately human nature, as a whole, has remained unreconstructed. We are capable of great heights but are also still equally capable of great depths.

How then should one who is a true Marxist, one called on to unite all people and eliminate repression, receive the Gods on their return? One can struggle against their return, deny that they exercise the power they do, and claim that one more try will make the hope for revolution succeed. But modern social history, or the political record since the first Marxist inspired revolution, does not make this seem likely. Men and women can of course continue to dream about creating new worlds, but there is no longer any reason not to dream with the Gods once more as well as with revolutionary leaders. If a single theoretical option is too narrow and if it treats the world too simplistically, no program has the right to demand the exile of the Gods in the name of human improvement.

The Marxist should at least greet the Gods' return with respect if not with an amazement that they survived so long under exile. To be banned seemingly only enhanced their power. All of us should join the Marxist in experiencing awe over the fact that we have witnessed the Gods' return from exile in our own time. For so long it was not only unexpected but even unimaginable, because we felt we were about to change the face of human nature forever and religion with it. We must rethink our too-simple notions of progress and at the same time feel the excitement which complexity brings as it challenges our powers to cope. Simple solutions and single courses of action when coupled with a necessity in nature are easier to handle. The return of the Gods signals a return to freedom, to uncertainty, to the excitement of an unknown that often transcends our grasp. But it is also a challenge once again to locate an acceptable God for our time from among the many Gods who crowd into our spiritual life.

Michael C. Brannigan

EVERYWHERE AND NOWHERE
The Path of Alan Watts

American University Studies: Series V (Philosophy). Vol. 54
ISBN 0-8204-0663-5   204 pages   hardback US $ 33.00*

*Recommended price – alterations reserved

The works of Alan Watts have had an undeniably profound impact upon contemporary Western culture. More than any other person, he has inspired the continued widespread interest in Oriental thought. His interpretation of Eastern viewpoints, especially from Zen Buddhism, provides the background for his own unique philosophy, which centers around the quest for individual identity. His path demands the radical transformation from our fragmented ego-conscious state to genuine self-awareness. As long as we remain under the spell of the ego, we maintain a counterfeit relationship with self and others, perpetuating a life-long struggle against nature, time, and death. Only when we break the chains of the illusion of ego, can we set out on the bridge to self-realization and discover who we truly are.

«... this eminently readable commentary on Watts' version of Eastern philosophy not only makes the latter accessible to a wider audience, it also contributes to building the bridge between philosophies and cultures.» (Joseph A. Selling, Professor, Katholieke Universiteit Leuven, Chairman, Department of Moral Theology)

«Here for the first time we have a critical study of (Watts') thought . . . Brannigan gives us a systematic exposition of Watts' positions and at the same time a critical evaluation that can help us understand the role he played in the meeting of East and West.» (Ewert Cousins, Fordham University)

PETER LANG PUBLISHING, INC.
62 West 45th Street
USA – New York, NY 10036

Emmanuel K. Twesigye

THE GLOBAL HUMAN PROBLEM
Ignorance, Hate, Injustice and Violence

American University Studies: Series VII (Theology and Religion). Vol. 48
ISBN 0-8204-0753-4   324 pages   hardback US $ 42.50*

*Recommended price – alterations reserved

The Global Human Problem: Ignorance, Hate, Injustice and Violence is a detailed philosophical-theological and axiological study, analysis and exposition of the global quintessential unique nature of the human being as God's special creature in the whole of the known cosmos. Characteristically, the author identifies the uniqueness of the human being with the human being's more developed and complex mental, linguistic, creative, moral and spiritual capacities which distinguish the human being as God's special creature and concrete moral representative agent or ambassador in God's creation. Subsequently, the author identifies the human reason for being in the world as that of stewardship, namely, taking loving care of all creation as well as one another, regardless of race, color, nationality, creed, ideology or gender. Consequently, prejudice, hate and war are all equally repudiated.
«It is an informative and thought-provoking book for students, scholars and practitioners who share a concern for the problem of the global human family and who wish to do something about ist.»

Anthony J. Nimley
Fisk University

PETER LANG PUBLISHING, INC.
62 West 45th Street
USA – New York, NY 10036

DATE DUE
